Queen Victoria

Icon of an Era

By Michael W. Simmons

Table of Contents

Chapter One: The Princess-in-Waiting (1819-1837)

The race for an heir

On May 24th, 1819, an infant daughter was born to the Duke and Duchess of Kent at Kensington Palace, one of the residences of the royal family of Britain. Her birth marked the end of a frantic two-year race between the many sons of King George III to produce a legitimate heir for the royal succession. Though the king was still living in 1819, his eldest son had ruled the country as Prince Regent since 1811, a substitution made necessary by the fact that George III suffered from prolonged periods of mental incapacity—that is, madness—due to what is believed to have been an untreated case of porphyria.

For many years, there had been an heir. The Prince Regent's only child was the beautiful, intelligent, much admired Princess Charlotte. The Princess's succession to the throne was eagerly anticipated by the British people, as her father and her uncles were immensely unpopular. The Prince Regent was a spendthrift who ran up fantastic debts, and his lavish appetites and huge size made him a cartoonish figure of gross consumption. His most serious crime in the eyes of the nation was the fact he had abruptly and callously abandoned his wife, Caroline of Brunswick, shortly after Princess Charlotte's birth, and afterwards taken up residence with a mistress, Maria Fitzherbert. In comparison to her father, whom she despised, Princess Charlotte was considered a model of virtue, restraint, and good judgment. But disaster struck the royal family when Princess Charlotte suffered a stillbirth and died of postpartum hemorrhaging in November of 1817.

King George III had suffered great unhappiness in his childhood, owing to domestic upheavals in his parents' and grandparents' generation. His own great-grandmother had been caught having an extramarital affair, prompting her husband, King George I, to banish her; he is also believed to have killed her lover. He then extended his rage to his son, the future George II, who could nothing but wrong in his eyes. Though George II himself had a happy marriage, the domestic curse transferred itself to his relationship with his eldest son, Frederick, Prince of Wales, which so miserable and strained that the king professed himself happy when Frederick died, leaving the future George III heir to the throne.

As a young man, George III was deeply affected by this legacy of family discord; he determined that, when he was king, he would distinguish himself from his forebears in the eyes of his people by doing good and setting a virtuous example for the nation. Though the traditional path to glory for a king was military victories, George III believed that "Virtue, religion, joined to nobility of sentiment, will support a prince better and make a people happier than all the abilities of an Augustus with the heart of Tiberius." But despite these excellent intentions, his numerous children were driven to restlessness and rebelliousness by his controlling approach to parenthood. His daughters were not allowed to marry until they were considerably older than was usual for women of their time. Unhappy under the paternal eye, they demanded a household of their own as soon as their brother became Regent. George III's sons enjoyed greater freedom than his daughters, but their lives were also dictated by the Royal Marriages Act of 1772, which forbade them to marry, except by the king's permission, until they were 25, after which they had to gain the approval of Parliament in order to marry, or forfeit their rights of succession. This led to secret marriages, mistresses, and a large number of illegitimate children being born to the royal children, including to one of George III's daughters.

Partially as a result of the Royal Marriages Act, partly due to simple bad luck, Princess Charlotte was, at the time of her death, George III's only legitimate grandchild. There was no shortage of heirs presumptive, since the king had twelve children living, but they were all middle-aged; it was therefore essential to secure the succession into the next generation. None of the married princesses had children, however, and as the youngest of them was already forty, there was no chance that they would become pregnant in the future. It was therefore up to the sons, who were a fairly dissolute bunch, to make marriages and produce children. The Prince Regent had divorced his wife and married his mistress, so there was no hope of more children from him. The Duke of York, Prince Frederick, was living apart from his wife and spent all of his time with his own mistress. The Duke of Clarence, who would succeed his brother as King William IV, had ten children with his mistress, but no legitimate issue. The Duke of Kent was living in Canada with *his* mistress. The Duke of Sussex had removed himself from the succession by marrying without permission, the Duke of Cambridge was unmarried, and the Duke of Cumberland, who had married in 1815, had no children.

After the death of Princess Charlotte, those of the royal dukes who were in a position to marry promptly ditched their mistresses, who had been their devoted companions for decades, and started hunting for wives, preferably wealthy ones. The British royal family was quite poor compared to most members of the aristocracy, and they depended on Parliamentary allowances for their income—allowances that were never large enough for their extravagant tastes. But the manufacturing heiresses of England refused to marry any of their royal suitors, so the sons of George III turned to the German states, which had been supplying brides to the royal families of Europe and Russia since the eighteenth century. The Duke of Clarence married Princess Adelaide of Saxe-Meiningen; the Duke of Cambridge married Princess Augusta of Hesse-Cassel.

This left the Duke of Kent, then living in Belgium with his mistress of twenty-four years, a French-Canadian woman called Madame St. Laurent. The Duke himself described his thoughts after the death of Princess Charlotte and the nature of his relationship with St. Laurent in a private conversation with a Mr. Creevey, who recorded the Duke's remarks in a diary without his knowledge. The whole exchange is related by Lytton Strachey in his early biography of Queen Victoria:

"Should the Duke of Clarence not marry," [the Duke of Kent] said, "the next prince in succession is myself, and although I trust I shall be at all times ready to obey any call my country may make upon me, God only knows the sacrifice it will be to make, whenever I shall think it my duty to become a married man. It is now seven and twenty years that Madame St. Laurent and I have lived together: we are of the same age, and have been in all climates, and in all difficulties together, and you may well imagine, Mr. Creevey, the pang it will occasion me to part with her. I put it to your own feelings—in the event of any separation between you and Mrs. Creevey... As for Madame St. Laurent herself, I protest I don't know what is to become of her if a marriage is to be forced upon me; her feelings are already so agitated upon the subject." The Duke went on to describe how, one morning, a day or two after the Princess Charlotte's death, a paragraph had appeared in the Morning Chronicle, alluding to the possibility of his marriage. He had received the newspaper at breakfast together with his letters, and "I did as is my constant practice, I threw the newspaper across the table to Madame St. Laurent, and began to open and read my letters. I had not done so but a very short time, when my attention was called to an extraordinary noise and a strong convulsive movement in Madame St. Laurent's throat. For a short time I entertained serious apprehensions for her safety; and when, upon her recovery, I enquired into the occasion of this attack, she pointed to the article in the Morning Chronicle."

Madame St. Laurent's agitations would prove to be warranted, for the Duke, not without some regret, was shortly to leave her flat. While still in Belgium, he applied to the widowed husband of Princess Charlotte, Prince Leopold of Saxe-Coburg, for a letter of introduction to his sister, Princess Marie Luise Victoria. Called Victoire by her family, the Princess of Saxe-Coburg was a widow, the mother of two young children: a son, Charles, and a daughter, Feodore. Lytton Strachey describes Princess Victoire as she appeared at the time: "thirty-two years old–short, stout, with brown eyes and hair, and rosy cheeks, cheerful and voluble, and gorgeously attired in rustling silks and bright velvets." She was regent of Amorbach in Lower Franconia since the death of her husband, the Prince of Leiningen, but despite her rank she was not comfortably situated. The recent wars had reduced the entire region and all those in it, including the ducal family, to a state of near-starvation. Royal though she was, she had nothing but her children to comfort her.

It had been suggested to the princess shortly after her first husband's death that she consider marriage with the Duke of Kent, but she had declined at the time, citing her duties as regent. But after the death of Princess Charlotte, the Duke became a far more attractive suitor. If she married him, there was a strong chance that her next child would be the future king or queen or England, which would mean considerable support from Parliament after the union and the promise of royal privileges to come. As it happened, the new allowance given to the Duke of Kent after his engagement was miserly in comparison to those given to his older brothers, but it seemed princely enough to Princess Victoire, coming as she did from aristocratic penury. The Duke of Kent and Princess Victoire were married in the summer of 1818, first in Coburg, then in a second ceremony in England. Victoire spoke very little English, so her wedding speech was written out for her phonetically with English words spelled with German and French letter combinations.

A royal household

It was not only the Duke's financial situation that appealed to the newlywed Duchess; though he was twenty years older than her and bald, well past his prime, the couple seemed, at least to outsiders, to get along very well and to take pleasure in one another's company. It was one of those rare occasions in which a marriage born of utility and politics blossoms into something more. Their daughter was born within a year of their union, and the birth was heralded as the arrival of "another Charlotte" by Victoire's mother: "The English like Queens, and the niece of the ever-lamented beloved Charlotte will be very dear to them." (This idea, that the English preferred queens to kings, became even more prevalent after Victoria's reign, and was often remarked upon after the accession of Elizabeth II in 1952.)

Alexandrina Victoria was christened in the Cupola Room of Kensington Palace on June 24, 1819. It took some time to settle on an appropriate name for the newborn infant. Everyone in the family had an opinion. Her father the Duke of Kent wished to name her Elizabeth. The Prince Regent, however, had determined that Tsar Alexander I of Russia should be her godfather, and that she should be named Alexandrina in his honor and Georgiana in honor of her grandfather, the King of England. But George III refused to play second fiddle to a foreign monarch, so at the last minute "Georgiana" was dropped. The substitution of

"Victoria", in honor of the baby's mother, was almost an afterthought. Victoria is now seen as a quintessentially English name, but that is because so many girls born during Victoria's reign were named in her honor. By contrast, when Victoria herself was christened, the name was seen as foreign, almost jarringly so. During her infancy she was called Drina for short.

The Duke, the Duchess, and their beloved infant daughter lived together happily for the next six months or so. When she was one month old, Drina received a smallpox vaccination, making her the first member of the royal family to undergo what was then a relatively new and controversial medical procedure. By the time she was a toddler, her family had taken to calling her Victoria. The Duke of Kent was of the firm opinion that he would ascend to the throne long before his young daughter. "My brothers are not so strong as I am," he had declared. "I have lived a regular life. I shall outlive them all. The crown will come to me and my children." But in January of 1820 the Duke caught a cold which rapidly developed into pneumonia, and on the 23rd of that month, he died. Only six days later his father, King George III, died as well, after a long final illness in which his dementia returned and he exhausted himself by talking for 58 hours straight. He was by this time alienated from much of his family, and his deathbed was attended by only one of his sons, Frederick, Duke of York.

The Prince Regent, already 57 years old, succeeded to the throne as George IV; he would live for another ten years, to be succeeded by his 64-year old brother, the Duke of Clarence, as William IV in 1830. For a time, it seemed as though the next heir to the throne would be the child of Clarence and his wife Princess Adelaide; though their first child, Princess Elizabeth, died shortly after birth, Adelaide was young and Clarence was strong, and there seemed every likelihood that they would have more children. But by the time George IV became king, it was apparent to everyone that no more children would be born to him or any of the other surviving sons of George III. Princess Victoria of Kent thus came to be regarded as the heiress presumptive, the future Queen of England. The persons responsible for the young princess's upbringing never forgot her royal destiny for an instant; every decision made on her behalf, every lesson she was taught, and every person she was allowed to socialize with was selected in the knowledge that they would play a role in shaping the character of a future monarch.

Educating a royal heir

For much of European history, the prevailing philosophy of government held that national stability was best achieved by concentrating power in the hands of a single family—a family founded by one exceptional person, whose descendants, it was hoped, would share some or all of his exceptional qualities. This belief was challenged by the rise of republican movements in Europe in the late eighteenth and early nineteenth century, as modern science began to diverge as a field of study distinct from theology, but the roots of this belief run deep, as evidenced by the fact that monarchy is anything but extinct in contemporary Europe.

Historically, England is one of only a few countries that allowed daughters to inherit the throne in the absence of sons, though elder daughters were second to younger brothers in the line of succession. Only recently did birth order supersede male primogeniture in royal inheritance laws. Just prior to the birth of Prince George of Cambridge in 2013, new laws were passed stating that the firstborn child of the present Duke and Duchess of Cambridge would take his or her place in the line of succession immediately after the Duke of Cambridge, regardless of the child's gender.

Throughout English history, even when a royal princess was born heiress presumptive (the "presumptive" qualifier indicates that there is a chance that she might be pre-empted in the succession by the birth of a younger brother), efforts were often made to bypass her for a more distant male relative with, arguably, less right by blood to the throne. This was especially the case before the Bill of Rights of 1689 and the Act of Settlement of 1701, which placed unprecedented limits on the monarch's power. A female monarch who wielded supreme power was seen as a danger to the security of the country, both because women were considered unequal to the task of supreme rule, and because there was never any telling what sort of person she might marry. The first queen regnant of England, Mary I, married Philip, King of Spain, which deeply displeased her subjects, who saw the marriage as equivalent to foreign rule. Immediately upon the accession of Mary's sister and successor, Elizabeth I found herself under immense pressure to marry someone—whether he be an English noble or a distant foreign king—because her youth and perceived feminine flightiness seemed to spell disaster for the future of the country. But Elizabeth rejected all of her suitors for reasons which, we will see later, also concerned Queen Victoria: she had been controlled all her life, and she enjoyed the power and independence that came with being Queen. If she had married, then Queen or not, she would have been expected to defer to her husband's authority. Elizabeth was too fond of her independence to place her crowned head in the matrimonial yoke. Victoria was nearly as reluctant to do so as her distant predecessor.

Victoria's case was otherwise unlike Elizabeth's. In an age of constitutional monarchy, her eventual succession to the throne was regarded as a blessing. Like the prematurely deceased Princess Charlotte, Victoria was looked upon as a figure of hope and renewal, a princess who promised a future free from the madness, the distasteful excesses, and the immoral conduct of her grandfather, father, and "bad uncles". As her grandmother wisely inferred, all the hopes that had been attached to Princess Charlotte were transferred to Princess Victoria upon her birth. Though Victoria came of the same Hanoverian bloodline as the mad king and his gouty son, she was female, and thus, according to the thinking of the time, inherently more virtuous than her male relatives. Moreover, it was thought certain that she would be carefully reared, preserved from corrupting influences, and thoroughly prepared for her future duties.

Traditionally, this was the other strength of the monarchial system—when power was concentrated in the hands of a single family and passed down from parent to child, the future monarch could be identified at birth and prepared from infancy for the daunting work that would consume their entire adult life. *Only* persons who had been born royal and received this life-long training could hope to wield those responsibilities capably, or so the thinking went. The theory was sound, but the practice often exposed the weaknesses rather than the strengths of the monarchial system. For one thing, there was no guarantee that the child of a strong and capable king would be strong and capable him or herself. Genetics don't always work that way. The descendants of a gifted leader may themselves be less intelligent, less emotionally stable, less sound of mind or body. These deficiencies may occur naturally; but very often, they are the byproduct of the training and education that was supposed to make them fit for their high office.

Monarchs historically have troubled relationships with their heirs. The heir to the throne is a constant reminder to the monarch that one day he or she will die, replaced by the same young person they are expected to regard with a parent's affection. And as the heir grows older, the monarch cannot help but regard him or her with some suspicion. Perhaps the heir will grow tired of waiting for his father to die in the due course of nature; perhaps he will come to think that he could rule the country better. More worryingly, there is a chance that he will make friends with opportunistic persons who whisper these suggestions to him in private, either out of a desire to curry favor, or because they serve a radical political agenda. More than once in European history, a monarch has grown so unpopular with his subjects that they plot to replace him, via assassination or coup. In such cases, the heir to the throne often makes a convenient figurehead for the revolutionary movement. (The Glorious Revolution of 1688 deposed the Catholic James II in favor of his Protestant daughter Mary and her husband Prince William of Orange; James and his entourage fled to France, and William and Mary were invited to become co-monarchs of England.)

However dutiful an heir may be to his kingly parent, however far from his or her thoughts any idea of rebellions or coups, there is always a chance that others may plot against the king behind both their backs, intending to present the heir with a fait accompli once their royal parent has already been beheaded or confined in a dungeon. These not unreasonable paranoias sometimes lead the monarch to undermine the very person whom they are supposed to be preparing to succeed them. They might neglect their child's education, treat him harshly or abusively, keep him isolated in order to prevent him from making friends who would support him or plot on his behalf. Or they might simply find it difficult to love the child who represents their own eventual demise, leading to emotional starvation of a kind that results in psychological instability later in life.

Only some of these factors influenced the upbringing of Princess Victoria of Kent, whose prematurely deceased father was a royal duke rather than a king, although the difficult relationship between monarchs and their heirs would come to be illustrated by Victoria's relationship with her own eldest son in the fullness of time. The larger point is merely that a child like Victoria, who is born to be queen, may enjoy unimaginable privilege and luxury in their early life, but they often face their own unique set of hardships and tribulations. From the moment of their birth, they have a target on their back, a bulls-eye with the potential to draw fire from any opportunistic person who sees the vulnerable child as someone to be influenced and controlled, or as a vehicle for their own ambition.

In Victoria's case, the opportunistic person who managed to insert himself into her mother's famously small and isolated household was a man by the name of Sir John Conroy. His desire to wield power through the girl who would one day be Queen of England led to considerable unhappiness in the princess's childhood.

The Kensington System

Sir John Conroy first came to be a part of the Duke of Kent's household when he was appointed as the Duke's equerry shortly before his marriage to Princess Victoire. Over time, he became more and more indispensable to the ducal family, especially to the Duchess. But his motivations were rooted in ambition, rather than service. This became evident during the Duke's last illness, when Conroy asked to be named as the sole guardian of the six-month old Princess Victoria. The Duke, naturally, refused, but once he was dead Conroy swiftly positioned himself as the comptroller of the widowed Duchess's household. She came to depend upon him absolutely, both because she felt herself to be in need of male guidance, and because it was difficult for her to interact with wider English society, as she still spoke little English. Conroy was valuable to the Duchess in many ways, but the influence he exerted through her over Victoria would ultimately destroy Victoria's relationship with her mother.

No one could be certain at what age Victoria might succeed to the throne. Her uncles were all in late middle age, and though the Duke of Clarence, the current heir presumptive, was said to be robust, he was nearer sixty than fifty. There was, therefore, a reasonable chance that Victoria would become queen when she was still a child. If this should turn out to be the case, a regent would have to be appointed for her until she reached the age of majority. Conroy's ultimate ambition was to have the Duchess of Kent named regent for her daughter. Since he was already the Duchess's most valued confidante and advisor, Conroy would then effectively control the monarch's own household.

Even an under-aged monarch might challenge Conroy's authority, however, particularly if she turned out to be a willful teenager, so Conroy set out to render Victoria isolated, unaccustomed to taking any action without first consulting himself or her mother. To achieve this, he devised a set of rules that were to govern every aspect of the princess's life until she was eighteen years old. This set of rules was referred to as the Kensington System. Biographer A.N. Wilson describes the System as an attempt to "bring up the princess detached from the English Court and her English uncles, and to be utterly dependent upon the Duchess of Kent and Conroy. But chiefly upon Conroy."

The decision to keep Victoria away from the influence of her royal relatives was not in itself an unreasonable one, considering the fact that the Prince Regent was openly living with a woman who was not his wife. Furthermore, after his death, the Duchess of Kent found herself on increasingly bad terms with William IV, and it would undoubtedly have distressed Victoria had she not been sheltered from it. But Victoria was sheltered from more than just family feuds—she spent years of her early life effectively isolated from anyone who might have been a friend, or at least, anyone not hand-picked by John Conroy. Apart from Conroy, the Princess and the Duchess lived retiringly with an all-female entourage: Victoria's beloved governess,

Baroness Lehzen, the duchess's lady in waiting, Baroness Späth, and Feodore, Victoria's half sister, who left the household to be married in 1828, when Victoria was nine. Victoria was cossetted, even spoiled as an infant, surrounded by doting caregivers, but by the time Feodore left, she was old enough to feel the lack of companions closer to her own age. She played often with the daughters of visiting noblewomen and with Conroy's own daughters, but the strict control Conroy exerted over her social life made her playmates little more than vehicles for his continuing influence.

Apart from the tutors who came to give lessons for brief periods throughout the week, the only male figure with whom Victoria had any contact was Conroy. A nineteenth century history writing about Victoria's early life asserts that the great misfortune of her childhood lay in the fact that, once her mother's brother Leopold left England to become King of the Belgians, she had no father-figure in her life and no contact with men. But Conroy was a daily feature of her life, and there was no question that she vastly preferred the company and guidance of women, chiefly her beloved governess, Baroness Lehzen. The fact that Conroy and Lehzen despised one another— Conroy resenting any rivals for influence over the future queen, Lehzen disapproving of Conroy in general—probably only deepened the young Victoria's loyalty towards the one and antipathy towards the other. (After Conroy had been banished from Victoria's royal presence, his son referred to Lehzen as "that hypocritical and detestable bitch", so the depth of his animosity can easily be imagined.) Another male influence, perhaps one capable of counteracting the authority wielded by Conroy, might well have done Victoria good. But if her mother had not been a widowed foreigner in a strange land, she might have permitted Conroy less influence over her daughter, and Victoria might have enjoyed a much closer relationship with her English uncles, who for all their faults were very fond of her.

The truly damaging aspects of the Kensington System were invisible until they were exposed by Victoria herself after she had become queen and all but banished both her mother and the hated Conroy from her life. And yet, Conroy himself was always regarded by those outside the Kensington establishment with suspicion. The Duchess of Clarence, wife of the soon-to-be King William IV, wrote to the Duchess of Kent, warning her that it would be better if she did not allow Conroy to have "too much influence over you, but keep him in his place... He has never lived before in court circles or in society, so naturally he offends sometimes against the traditional ways, for he does not know them... In the family it is noticed that you are cutting yourself off more and more from them with your child... This they attribute to Conroy, whether rightly or wrongly I cannot judge." Princess Adelaide's judgment was astute; it was Conroy's design from the beginning to keep "the family" as far away from the young princess as he could manage. But as long as the Duchess of Kent chose to defend him, there was little that the Clarences, or even the king, could do.

The Kensington System is famous today primarily for its bizarre, even arbitrary rules pertaining to Victoria's movements. For instance, she was never permitted to be alone for a single moment during the day, and at night she was not permitted to sleep alone—her bed was therefore placed in the same room as her mother's. When Victoria ascended or descended staircases, she had to walk next to someone else and hold their arm. (In all fairness, there was a virtual epidemic in the 19th century of women tripping over their long skirts and breaking ankles, as well as more important bones, so this rule, however infantilizing, was probably aimed at making certain that Conroy's golden goose didn't break her neck before she became queen.) Vitoria was also forbidden to read novels or any other literature that had not been approved by her guardians. So far these restrictions seem calculated to produce the opposite effect from what Conroy intended—surely any young person would eventually chafe and rebel against such rules. But the System had its benefits as well, rules that a sensible girl like Victoria would find it difficult to justify revolting against. These included a regular academic schedule, with lessons beginning promptly at 9:30, ending in a break at 11:30, and recommencing in the afternoon.

Lytton Strachey writes that,

"The Duchess felt convinced that it was her supreme duty in life to make quite sure that her daughter should grow up into a Christian queen. To this task she bent all her energies; and, as the child developed, she flattered herself that her efforts were not unsuccessful. When the Princess was eleven, she desired the Bishops of London and Lincoln to submit her daughter to an examination, and report upon the progress that had been made.

"'I feel the time to be now come,' the Duchess explained, in a letter obviously drawn up by her own hand, 'that what has been done should be put to some test, that if anything has been done in error of judgment it may be corrected, and that the plan for the future should be open to consideration and revision... I attend almost always myself every lesson, or a part; and as the lady about the Princess is a competent person, she assists Her in preparing Her lessons, for the various masters, as I resolved to act in that manner so as to be Her Governess myself. When she was at a proper age she commenced attending Divine Service regularly with me, and I have every feeling that she has religion at Her heart, that she is morally impressed with it to that degree, that she is less liable to error by its application to her feelings as a Child capable of reflection.'

'"The general bent of Her character,' added the Duchess, 'is strength of intellect, capable of receiving with ease, information, and with a peculiar readiness in coming to a very just and benignant decision on any point Her opinion is asked on. Her adherence to truth is of so marked a character that I feel no apprehension of that Bulwark being broken down by any circumstances.'"

Strachey goes on to describe the interview which, according to the Duchess's wishes, took place between the Bishops and the young princess when Victoria was eleven years old:

"The Bishops attended at the Palace, and the result of their examination was all that could be wished. 'In answering a great variety of questions proposed to her,' they reported, 'the Princess displayed an accurate knowledge of the most important features of Scripture History, and of the leading truths and precepts of the Christian Religion as taught by the Church of England, as well as an acquaintance with the Chronology and principal facts of English History remarkable in so young a person. To questions in Geography, the use of the Globes, Arithmetic, and Latin Grammar, the answers which the Princess returned were equally satisfactory.' They did not believe that the Duchess's plan of education was susceptible of any improvement; and the Archbishop of Canterbury, who was also consulted, came to the same gratifying conclusion."

It is worth pointing out that the points on which Victoria was being examined were predominantly related to theology, with a secondary emphasis on the usual schoolroom subjects of English history, geography, and basic arithmetic. She was also said to have a facility for languages, including Latin, Italian, French, and German. But there was one glaring omission in this curriculum, considering the career it was meant to be preparing her for. At no time was Princess Victoria drilled in matters pertaining to law, politics, or government, and the omission nearly led to disastrous consequences in the first three years of her reign, before she was taken in hand by more experienced persons. (As a point of interest, Victoria's great-granddaughter, Elizabeth II, was tutored in precisely the reverse curriculum: almost all the normal school subjects were neglected in her education, but matters of Constitutional law and government were drilled into her by a professor at Eton college when she was a child.)

One reason for this omission was that Victoria was not yet aware that she was due to inherit the throne of England, and she would not be told until the year after her examination by the bishops, when she was twelve. The Duchess had explained to the bishops that she was still ignorant with regards to her future fate, lest they should say something to the princess that would lead to her asking awkward questions. But the Duchess also assured them that the groundwork for the inevitable revelation had been established: "She is aware of [the monarch's] duties, and that a Sovereign should live for others; so that when Her innocent mind receives the impression of Her future fate, she receives it with a mind formed to be sensible of what is to be expected from Her, and it is to be hoped, she will be too well grounded in Her principles to be dazzled with the station she is to look to."

The circumstances under which Princess Victoria came to realize that she was one day to be Queen were already legendary by the time biographers were writing the first histories of her life. Lytton Strachey alludes to "the well-known scene":

"...The history lesson, the genealogical table of the Kings of England slipped beforehand by the governess into the book, the Princess's surprise, her inquiries, her final realization of the facts. When the child at last understood, she was silent for a moment, and then she spoke: "I will be good," she said. The words were something more than a conventional protestation, something more than the expression of a superimposed desire; they were, in their limitation and their intensity, their egotism and their humility, an instinctive summary of the dominating qualities of a life."

"I will be good" did, in fact, mean something particular coming from the twelve-year-old princess, who had heard vague but troubling rumors all her life about the "bad" behavior of her royal uncles. The careful moral and religious instruction that Victoria received as a child was partly due to 19th century societal norms, partly due to the character of her pious mother and her governess (Baroness Lehzen was the daughter of a German pastor), and partly due to the fact that Victoria herself was of the Hanoverian line. The royal side of her family came of a bloodline that often manifested problematic personality flaws: deep passions, ungovernable fits of temper, stubbornness, and excess. The principle examples of these undesirable family traits were found in George III, who died mad, and in George IV, who was licentious to a fault. Nor was Victoria's own father, the Duke of Kent, an exception to the Hanoverian weaknesses. The Duke boasted of having lived "a regular life" in contrast to his brothers—meaning that he had a military career and a fairly conventional domestic situation, if one overlooks the fact that for most of his life he lived with a mistress, not a wife. But in military circles the Duke of Kent was known as a notorious martinet who flogged his men to the point of unconsciousness for the slightest infractions. At one stage in his career, he had to be removed from his post, because his disciplinary methods were so harsh that it was feared his men would be driven to mutiny.

There is no doubt that Victoria was closely watched throughout her life by those who feared that the family demons would manifest themselves in the young girl. Her caregivers had some reason to be concerned; as a small child Victoria had been prone to frightful tantrums, inspiring one of her attendants to remark that she was "George III in petticoats". Even when she had outgrown these tantrums, she was a person of deep passions who hated and loved extravagantly. She only listened to persons whom she loved, as Baroness Lehzen discovered when she first set out to teach the five-year old Victoria how to read. Every attempt to teach Victoria the alphabet prior to the age of five had failed, but when Baroness Lehzen was made her governess, she quickly realized that once she had secured the child's affections, Victoria would do anything to please her, including her homework. It is no wonder, therefore, that John Conroy despised the Baroness; if he ever tried to secure Victoria's affections, he certainly failed. There would come a moment when she was about sixteen when Conroy would ask Victoria for the prize he had been working towards since the moment she was born. Her refusal should have come as no surprise to him; but from everything that we now know about Conroy, it could not be plainer that he did not understand Victoria at all, nor ever had.

Victoria the diarist

Victoria is a fascinating subject of biographical study, not merely because of the remarkable life she led, but because she herself had a penchant for autobiography. From the age of thirteen onwards she kept a daily diary. As a young teenager, her diary was an outlet for a lonely girl who had few other confidantes, written in the awareness that her mother, and possibly Conroy and Lehzen, would certainly read it. While Victoria's guardians never scrupled to breach her privacy, this was not the betrayal of trust it might seem. Up until the late nineteenth century, most people who kept diaries wrote them in the expectation that other people would read them eventually. A person's diary might be published, if they happened to be a particularly good writer, or their family might pick them up and read them at any time. It wasn't until the turn of the century, when stationers began selling blank books equipped with small locks, that diaries and journals began to be conceived of as private, confidential documents.

Even when she was an adult and Queen, no longer a powerless, friendless girl, Victoria kept up with her diaries, writing many thousands of words a day in them, pouring all the private feelings that a public figure could not easily express onto the page. These diaries, too, would be read one day—the diaries of a Queen, after all, are historical documents as well as private ones. They were, however, heavily redacted after Victoria's death by her children, who removed any content that seemed too private—such as criticisms of living persons (especially family members), or opinions and anecdotes that might contradict the Queen's carefully cultivated public image as the most respectable and conventional of wives and mothers.

Nonetheless, the diary entries which have survived from Victoria's childhood paint a portrait of a bright, enthusiastic, inquisitive child who possessed deep feelings and thought seriously on the milestones of her young life. In one entry, she reflects on her confirmation ceremony, and her thoughts are much preoccupied by the solemnity of the occasion, with only a slight digression onto the new dress she received for the occasion:

"I felt that my confirmation was one of the most solemn and important events and acts in my life; and that I trusted that it might have a salutary effect on my mind. I

felt deeply repentant for all what I had done which was wrong and trusted in God Almighty to strengthen my heart and mind; and to forsake all that is bad and follow all that is virtuous and right. I went with the firm determination to become a true Christian, to try and comfort my dear Mamma in all her griefs, trials, and anxieties, and to become a dutiful and affectionate daughter to her. Also to be obedient to DEAR Lehzen, who has done so much for me. I was dressed in a white lace dress, with a white crepe bonnet with a wreath of white roses round it. I went in the chariot with my dear Mamma and the others followed in another carriage."

The young Victoria took her studies seriously, but she was not a great reader. This was probably due to the fact that she was expressly forbidden to read novels, which were a fairly new art form in the 1820s and considered to be something less than wholly respectable. Instead, she was given dry volumes on poetry, philosophy, and religion to read, which are the sort of books that would probably fail to interest any thirteen-year old. (As an adult, Queen Victoria would become passionately fond of the novels of Sir Walter

Scott, so clearly her distaste for reading had less to do with an unwillingness to devote herself to such a quiet, studious task, and more to do with the tedious nature of the reading material she had access to). The books that she did read, she reviewed in her diaries. One one occasion, she somehow managed to lay her hands on a copy of the memoirs of British actress Fanny Kemble, which would by no means have been considered suitable reading even for a young girl from a less restrictive family. But Victoria was not impressed by the book's borderline salacious content:

"It is certainly very pertly and oddly written. One would imagine by the style that the authoress must be very pert, and not well bred; for there are so many vulgar expressions in it. It is a great pity that a person endowed with so much talent, as Mrs. Butler really is, should turn it to so little account and publish a book which is so full of trash and nonsense which can only do her harm. I stayed up till 20 minutes past 9."

The Bishop of Chester's *Exposition of the Gospel of St. Matthew* received much higher praise in Victoria's diary: "It is a very fine book indeed. Just the sort of one I like; which is just plain and comprehensible and full of truth and good feeling. It is not one of those learned books in which you have to cavil at almost every paragraph. Lehzen gave it me on the Sunday that I took the Sacrament [i.e. at her confirmation]."

Victoria's teenage diaries were not so different from the diaries that a girl of the same age might have written at virtually any point in modern history. Which is to say that in addition to containing commentary on the books she was reading and the new clothes she received, they also contained detailed appraisals of the few young men who made appearances in her tight-knit family circle. When she was fourteen, she met her cousins, Prince Alexander and Prince Ernst of Württemberg, the sons of her mother's sister. Her diary proclaims that: "They are both EXTREMELY TALL, Alexander is VERY HANDSOME, and Ernst has a VERY KIND EXPRESSION. They are both extremely AMIABLE." When their visit was concluded, she seemed to feel their loss keenly: "We saw them get into the barge, and watched them sailing away for some time on the beach. They were so amiable and so pleasant to have in the house; they were ALWAYS SATISFIED, ALWAYS GOOD-HUMOURED; Alexander took such care of me in getting out of the boat, and rode next to me; so did Ernst."

Two years after the departure of the Württemberg princes, the family was visited by more of Victoria's cousins, the Princes Ferdinand and Augustus:

"Dear Ferdinand has elicited universal admiration from all parties... He is so very unaffected, and has such a very distinguished appearance and carriage. They are both very dear and charming young men. Augustus is very amiable, too, and, when known, shows much good sense. On another occasion, Dear Ferdinand came and sat near me and talked so dearly and sensibly. I do SO love him. Dear Augustus sat near me and talked with me, and he is also a dear good young man, and is very handsome... On the whole, I think Ferdinand handsomer than Augustus, his eyes are so beautiful, and he has such a lively clever expression; BOTH have such a sweet expression; Ferdinand has something QUITE BEAUTIFUL in his expression when he speaks and smiles, and he is SO good... [They were] both very handsome and VERY DEAR."

Some three years later, Victoria would make the acquaintance of another pair of handsome young cousins who would sweep all memory of Ferdinand and Augustus from her mind.

The "royal progresses" and conflict with William IV

As Princess Victoria approached her later teens, the Duchess of Kent, encouraged by John Conroy, began to take up the attitude that her privileges as the mother of the future Queen of England were being insufficiently recognized by King William IV and the court of Windsor. Without wishing to change her actual title, the Duchess believed that she was entitled to all the honors, precedence, and monies normally accorded to a Dowager Princess of Wales. Her logic was somewhat convoluted. "Prince of Wales" is the title traditionally granted to the monarch's eldest son and heir; therefore, the Princess of Wales tended to be the mother of the person next in line for the throne after her husband. But the Duchess of Kent was the widow of William IV's brother, not his son, and while her daughter Victoria was widely regarded as the heir apparent, the king himself had not yet given up all hope of having a child of his own before he died. Needless to say, he found the Duchess's claims annoying and specious.

The Duchess annoyed him still further when she and Conroy elected to take Princess Victoria on a series of tours across England when she was a young teenager. The primary purpose of the tours was to introduce the future queen to the realm she was one day to govern and give the people an opportunity to glimpse her. But it also served the secondary purpose of glorifying the Duchess, which annoyed William IV to no end. Lytton Strachey describes the King's reaction:

"It was advisable that Victoria should become acquainted with the various districts of England, and through several summers a succession of tours–in the West, in the Midlands, in Wales–were arranged for her. The intention of the plan was excellent, but its execution was unfortunate. The journeys, advertised in the Press, attracting enthusiastic crowds, and involving official receptions, took on the air of royal progresses. Addresses were presented by loyal citizens, the delighted Duchess, swelling in sweeping feathers and almost obliterating the diminutive Princess, read aloud, in her German accent, gracious replies prepared beforehand by Sir John, who, bustling and ridiculous, seemed to be mingling the roles of major-domo and Prime Minister. Naturally the King fumed over his newspaper at Windsor. 'That woman is a nuisance!' he exclaimed."

At the Duchess's insistence, nearby ships fired full royal gun salutes when the princess's party arrived in a district. William IV responded by firing off an irritable royal edict of his own, stating that no royal gun salute was ever to be given save in the presence of the monarch himself, or in the presence of his consort. The Duchess seethed, but could do nothing about it.

The conflict between the Duchess's establishment at Kensington and the royal household at Windsor had been ongoing for years, but Victoria had been sheltered from any knowledge of the animosity between the two sides of her family when she was a child. She had no idea, for instance, that at one time the king had considered removing her from Kensington Palace and bring her to Windsor to be brought up. But the older she grew, the more impossible it became to keep her in ignorance. When she was seventeen, her mother's brother, Leopold, King of Belgium, came to visit William IV at Windsor and was met with a decidedly frosty reception. Victoria, unconscious of the King's displeasure, was delighted to see her mother's broter, writing in her diary that:

"To hear dear Uncle speak on any subject is like reading a highly instructive book; his conversation is so enlightened, so clear. He is universally admitted to be one of the first politicians now extant. He speaks so mildly, yet firmly and impartially, about politics. Uncle tells me that Belgium is quite a pattern for its organisation, its industry, and prosperity; the finances are in the greatest perfection. Uncle is so beloved and revered by his Belgian subjects, that it must be a great compensation for all his extreme trouble."

During the same visit, William IV's irritation with the whole German side of Victoria's family manifested itself in an outburst over a formal dinner. The King of England confronted the King of the Belgians by demanding to know, "What's that you're drinking, sir?" Leopold replied, "Water, sir." "God damn it, sir!" William shouted. "Why don't you drink wine? I never allow anybody to drink water at my table."

Victoria's summer tours across England were more than a source of annoyance to her uncle the King—they were also beginning to wear on her health. By the end of her final tour of the north in 1835, she was utterly exhausted and had to take to her bed with a cold. The cold developed into an "ulcerated sore throat"—probably strep throat, which was potentially fatal prior to the invention of modern antibiotics. Typhus was also a possible culprit. John Conroy, however, refused to believe that the princess was seriously sick. He downplayed the risk to her health, concerned that if too much was made of her her illness, the papers would get wind of it and trigger a political crisis. After all, if Victoria died, her uncle the Duke of Cumberland would become heir presumptive to the throne of England. Cumberland was a reactionary conservative, regarded as a menacing threat to the future of the country by the Whig factions, who numbered Conroy and the deceased Duke of Kent among their number. In the eyes of many, only Victoria stood between England and revolution.

Leopold of Belgium had joined the family at the Albion Hotel in Ramsgate when Victoria's tour came to an end. He took a far more serious view of Victoria's illness than Conroy did—understandably so, considering that his own wife, Princess Charlotte, had died under English medical care. "If in consequence of your folly anything happens to the princess, there is of course an end to all your prospects," he warned Conroy. "If the princess lives and succeeds the king, she will abhor you. Though late in the day, still things may be placed on a tolerable footing for you."

The timing of Leopold's remarks is unclear; when he spoke of Victoria "abhorring" Conroy, he may simply have been referring to Conroy's unkindness during her illness. But there was an incident which took place between Victoria and Conroy while she was confined to her sickbed that may also have prompted Leopold's warning. At some point while she was fighting for her life in that Ramsgate hotel room,

"...Conroy clumsily entered [Victoria's] bedroom and attempted to make her promise to ensure his position, and her mother's as Regent. She refused. It would seem that Conroy was all but violent with her. When the crisis in the illness had passed, his fate was sealed. Henceforward, her hatred of him was out in the open and, together with Lehzen and the King, she was merely waiting for the moment when she reached eighteen in order to be rid of Sir John and his influence. Conroy tried to force her to make him her official private secretary. She refused. 'And therein...lies the whole affair. With every day that she grew older the princess naturally became more aware of her self, more conscious of her own strength, and hence became jealous of what she must have seen as an exercise of undue control over herself.'"

If Leopold had known of Conroy's conduct towards Victoria during this incident (she was just sixteen years old at the time), one would think that he would do more than warn Conroy that he was turning Victoria against him. But Leopold may have been unwilling to interfere with Conroy for as long as his sister continued to rely upon his guidance. In any case, his warning was prescient: Victoria's hatred and abhorrence of Conroy only deepened from this point forward. As soon as she succeeded to the throne, she banished him from her life completely.

Marital prospects

The following year, when Victoria was seventeen, both her mother and her uncles began to think seriously of whom she ought to marry. The Duchess of Kent's wish was that Victoria marry her sister's son, Prince Ernest of Coburg. Accordingly, the Duchess invited Ernest and his brother Albert to England for a visit. William IV, however, had matchmaking tendencies of his own—he wanted Victoria to marry Prince

Alexander of Orange. Unaware that the Duchess had already invited her Coburg nephews to England, the king extended an invitation to Prince Alexander to come to Windsor and make Victoria's acquaintance. The King was apoplectic when he learned that the Duchess had invited Ernest and Albert without giving him notice, and he demanded that she cancel the invitation forthwith. This proved impossible, for the princes had already started out on their journey. They were already in London by the time Victoria was being introduced to Prince Alexander. But the prince of Orange proved stuffy, dull, and boring, and contrary to the King's hopes, Victoria was not interested in him in the slightest. "So much for the Oranges," she wrote to her uncle Leopold.

Prince Ernest of Coburg, along with his brother Albert and his father, Victoria's "Uncle Ernest", were received at Kensington shortly afterwards. Though Ernest was the ostensible star of this preliminary courting game, it was Albert, "a boy of almost shocking beauty, and of almost equally stunning seriousness and shyness" who caught Victoria's imagination when she first glimpsed him from the top of a staircase. Her diary spares no descriptive detail:

"Ernest is as tall as Ferdinand and Augustus; he has dark hair, and fine dark eyes and eyebrows, but the nose and mouth are not good; he has a most kind, honest, and intelligent expression in his countenance, and has a very good figure. Albert, who is just as tall as Ernest but stouter, is extremely handsome; his hair is about the same colour as mine; his eyes are large and blue, and he has a beautiful nose and a very sweet mouth with fine teeth; but the charm of his countenance is his expression, which is most delightful; c'est a la fois full of goodness and sweetness, and very clever and intelligent... Both my cousins are so kind and good; they are much more...men of the world than Augustus; they speak English very well, and I speak it with them. Ernest will be 18 years old on the 21st of June, and Albert 17 on the 26th of August. Dear Uncle Ernest made me the present of a most delightful Lory [lorikeet], which is so tame that it remains on your hand and you may put your finger into its beak, or do anything with it, without its ever attempting to bite. It is larger than Mamma's grey parrot."

"I sat between my dear cousins on the sofa and we looked at drawings. They both draw very well, particularly Albert, and are both exceedingly fond of music; they play very nicely on the piano. The more I see them the more I am

delighted with them, and the more I love them...
It is delightful to be with them; they are so fond
of being occupied too; they are quite an example
for any young person."

The depth of feeling which Victoria was already
beginning to cherish towards the younger of her
two Coburg cousins begins to grow apparent in
the diary entry she wrote following the departure
of himself, his brother, and his father from
Kensington:

"It was our last HAPPY HAPPY breakfast,
with this dear Uncle and those DEAREST
beloved cousins, whom I DO love so VERY VERY
dearly; MUCH MORE DEARLY than any other
cousins in the WORLD. Dearly as I love
Ferdinand, and also good Augustus, I love Ernest
and Albert MORE than them, oh yes, MUCH
MORE... They have both learnt a good deal, and
are very clever, naturally clever, particularly
Albert, who is the most reflecting of the two, and
they like very much talking about serious and
instructive things and yet are so VERY VERY
merry and gay and happy, like young people
ought to be; Albert always used to have some fun
and some clever witty answer at breakfast and
everywhere; he used to play and fondle Dash
[Victoria's dog] so funnily too... Dearest Albert

was playing on the piano when I came down. At 11 dear Uncle, my DEAREST BELOVED cousins, and Charles, left us, accompanied by Count Kolowrat. I embraced both my dearest cousins most warmly, as also my dear Uncle. I cried bitterly, very bitterly."

Ultimately, neither the Duchess nor the King were to prove victorious in uniting their chosen candidate to the princess—at least, not during this visit. Ernest, Albert, and Alexander were swiftly banished from her thoughts as more serious matters began to loom on the horizon of her small universe. Tension between William IV and the Duchess of Kent were escalating; and more significantly, the King's health was worsening. Victoria's thoughts were fixed on a future that did not include matrimony. Not yet, anyway.

The King's birthday

In August of 1836, four months after Victoria celebrated her seventeenth birthday in the company of Ernest and Albert of Coburg, she and her mother were invited to Windsor to celebrate the birthday of William IV. No sooner had the

Princess and the Duchess departed Kensington than the King took a brief trip to London to open Parliament, stopping in along the way to inspect conditions at Kensington Palace.

The palace was the dwelling of the Duchess's household, but it belonged to, and was paid for, by the Crown. The King, therefore, had a perfect right to make use of it when he wished. The Duchess had recently applied to the King for permission to take over an extravagant suite of seventeen rooms in a more luxurious wing of the palace, but he had denied the request, stating that he wished the rooms to be kept available for his own use. It therefore came as an outrageous shock to him when he discovered that the Duchess had ignored his orders and moving into the suite anyway. To the King, this was simply more evidence that the Duchess was determined to give herself airs above her station. By the time he returned to Windsor for his birthday dinner, he was bristling with the desire to put the Duchess in her place.

As soon as the King came face to face with the Kensington delegation, he greeted Princess Victoria "with affection", grasping her hands and expressing his deep regret that he had seen so little of her in recent years. Then he bowed to the

Duchess, and "publicly rebuked [her] for what she had done". He declared that "a most unwarrantable liberty had been taken with one of his Palaces; that He had just come from Kensington, where He found apartments had been taken possession of not only without his consent, but contrary to his commands and that he neither understood nor would endure conduct so disrespectful to him." The Duchess was, naturally, mortified. But the King had not yet fully vented his ire against her. His birthday banquet took place the next day, and after a long dinner and the free consumption of wine, the King rose to make a speech. Lytton Strachey sets the scene: "...There were a hundred guests; the Duchess of Kent sat on the King's right hand, and the Princess Victoria opposite. At the end of the dinner, in reply to the toast of the King's health, he rose, and, in a long, loud, passionate speech, poured out the vials of his wrath upon the Duchess."

The King's speech proceeded as follows:

"I trust in God that my life may be spared for the nine months longer, after which period, in the event of my death, no Regency would take place. I should then have the satisfaction of leaving the royal authority to the personal exercise of that Young Lady [pointing to the Princess], the Heiress Presumptive of the Crown, and not in the hands of the person now near me [the Duchess of Kent, seated to his right], who is surrounded by evil advisers and who is herself incompetent to act with propriety in the station in which She would be placed. I have no hesitation in saying that I have been insulted—grossly and continually insulted—by that person, but I am determined to endure no longer a course of behavior so disrespectful to me. Amongst many other things I have particularly to complain of the manner in which that young Lady has been kept away from my Court; she has been repeatedly kept from my drawing-rooms, at which she ought always to have been present, but I am fully resolved that this shall not happen again. I would have her know that I am King and that I am determined to make my authority respected."

The King ended his remarks by expressing deep paternal affection for Victoria herself. No doubt he felt slightly guilty for subjecting her to his outburst, for she had burst into tears. She was sensible enough to understand that her uncle's anger was not directed towards her, but she was likewise canny enough to know that any humiliation endured by her mother would spoil the atmosphere back home for weeks to come.

And the Duchess was more than humiliated—she was incensed beyond measured. Reportedly, she endured the King's rebuke and "said not a word until the tirade was over and the company had retired; then in a tornado of rage and mortification, she called for her carriage and announced her immediate return to Kensington. It was only with the utmost difficulty that some show of a reconciliation was patched up, and the outraged lady was prevailed upon to put off her departure till the morrow."

This was precisely the sort of domestic upheaval which had long characterized the royal Court of the Hanoverians, not only during the present generation, but extending as far back as King George I. It is there more understandable why Princess Victoria had always been kept at a distance from her English family; but now there was no more question of keeping her in ignorance. She would be eighteen before the year was out. The vultures were circling around her. Whom would she marry? Which advisers would she choose, and on whose advice would she rely? Did she have the education and strength of character to reign according to her own principles, or would England be at the mercy of whoever came to wield the greatest measure of influence over her? These were the questions the members of the aging King's court were asking

one another as the day of her accession drew
closer.

Chapter Two: The New Queen
(1837-1840)

The death of King William IV

On May 24, 1837, Princess Victoria satisfied the deepest wishes of herself and her uncle the King by turning eighteen while the King yet lived. William IV was gravely ill, but he would be able to die in peace, confident that his heir and successor had reached her majority. There were now no Constitutional grounds for requiring a Regency. A little over a year previously, Conroy had unwisely attempted to browbeat the Princess into appointing him her private secretary, which would give him almost unlimited control over the royal household. Furthermore, he had wanted her to agree to a regency until she had reached the age of twenty-five. Coming from Conroy, both of these demands were self-serving, but the latter suggestion was not entirely irrational. The first three years of Victoria's reign would demonstrate just how sheltered she really was; thanks to Conroy himself, she was less mature in some ways than other young women of eighteen. But Conroy had destroyed any influence he might ever have possessed over her by attempting to take advantage of her in her weakened state. As the King's health worsened and the day of Victoria's accession drew near, other politicians and ministers began to whisper about the possibility of a regency as well. But Conroy had destroyed their chances too. Nothing would make her consent to a regency now, no matter how young or ill-equipped to rule she might be.

There are interesting parallels between the young Victoria and her distant predecessor, Elizabeth, who was twenty-five when she succeeded her sister Mary I as Queen in 1558. As royal princesses, both Victoria and Elizabeth had been closely watched and controlled all their lives. And both women relished their sudden power and independence when they came to the throne. In Elizabeth's case, her unwillingness to marry was directly related to her fear of being once again subject to male authority. Victoria was hesitant to marry for the same reason—at least, until she fell head over heels in love. In any case, Victoria was deeply aware that Conroy and others wished to fit her with a regent as a horse is fitted with a bridle; it is therefore unsurprising that she was unwilling to entertain the prospect. After her 18th birthday, she began to defy the rules of the Kensington System, as if the knowledge that the day of her accession was not far off made her see the world with new eyes. When Victoria arrived at the birthday ball given by the King in her honor, she did alone, in her own carriage, with only an attendant for company. Her mother the Duchess traveled in the carriage directly behind hers; it was the first time Victoria had ever driven anywhere without her direct supervision.

William IV was equally eager that Victoria's birthday should signal the beginning of the changing of the guard: during the banquet, he seated her in his own chair of state at the high table, while the other members of the Kensington entourage were left to shift for seating amongst the rest of the guests. Both uncle and niece were sending a clear message: Victoria was a monarch-in-waiting, and her hangers-on were not eligible for the privileges that applied solely to her.

This did not, however, prevent Conroy from making a final attempt to grab power before all opportunity was lost. A day or two after Victoria's birthday celebrations, Baron Stockmar, family physician to the Coburg family, came to visit the princess with an inquiry: had she been aware that the Prime Minister, Lord Melbourne, had offered her a £10,000 increase in allowance as a birthday present from the King? More to the point, was Victoria aware that the Duchess, through John Conroy, had refused the gift in Victoria's name? No, Victoria, said, she had not been made aware of the King's offer, nor of her mother's refusal; she was incensed that such a decision had been made without her consent or knowledge. "Not only have I never seen or heard of this letter [containing Melbourne's offer]," she told Stockmar, "but I was never told by my Mother that Lord Melbourne had been here. As I never knew anything of Lord Melbourne's letter, I am, of course, also totally ignorant of the answer."

Stockmar had of course been aware that the whole affair had been carried on behind Victoria's back; his goal in bringing it to her attention was to weaken the last of Conroy's influence over her. His gambit was wisely chosen. Victoria swiftly pinned the blame on her mother's comptroller. The last thing she wanted, she explained to Stockmar, was to allow Conroy "any interference in my affairs. Whatever he has done, it has been done by order of my Mother...without making me responsible for any of her actions, as Sir John is her private secretary and neither my servant nor adviser, nor ever was."

By June 4 of 1837 it was clear that the King could not live for much longer. All normal business at Kensington Palace was suspended, for the princess could not concentrate on her lessons. Every hour of the day, she was on alert for a message from the palace, bearing the news that William IV was dead and she, Victoria, was now Queen of England. The suspense lasted for two more weeks; then, in the early hours of the morning on June 20, the King breathed his last, attended at his bedside by Queen Adelaide, the Archbishop of Canterbury, and the Lord Chamberlain, Lord Conyngham, the legitimate son of George IV's longtime mistress. The King had died at two in the morning. At five in the morning, the Archbishop and Lord Chamberlain arrived at Kensington Palace to bring the news to Victoria. "It was only with considerable difficulty that they gained admittance," writes Strachey. The Duchess of Kent would not consent to wake her daughter until 6 a.m., at which point:

"She got out of bed, put on her dressing-gown, and went, alone, into the room where the messengers were standing. Lord Conyngham fell on his knees, and officially announced the death of the King; the Archbishop added some personal details. Looking at the bending, murmuring dignitaries before her, she knew that she was Queen of England. 'Since it has pleased

Providence,' she wrote that day in her journal, 'to place me in this station, I shall do my utmost to fulfil my duty towards my country; I am very young, and perhaps in many, though not in all things, inexperienced, but I am sure, that very few have more real good will and more real desire to do what is fit and right than I have.'

Queen Victoria's first exercise of her royal authority was to read and reply to a letter from her aunt Adelaide, now the Queen Dowager, asking the new Queen's permission to remain at Windsor castle until after William IV's funeral had taken place. Victoria wrote back hastily, "begging her to consult nothing but her own health and convenience, and to remain at Windsor just as long as she pleases." She then gave the letter into the hands of the Lord Chamberlain and sent him back to Windsor to deliver it. The Archbishop of Canterbury then informed her that her uncle the King had died penitent and reconciled to God and the Church of England. Afterwards, he left her alone. That she be given half an hour alone was her first request as Queen; in her whole life, she had never been permitted to be entirely alone before. Afterwards, she decided to go back to bed. The second order she gave as Queen was for the servants to move her bed out of her mother's bedroom. She had never slept alone before, either.

The authority of the Duchess of Kent, Sir John Conroy, and their Kensington System was broken forever, and Conroy, at least, was swift to realize it. Now that Victoria was queen, Conroy prepared to collect such rewards as he could reasonably claim for having served the Kents for twenty years, and for "his past services to the ignorant little child that was called to preside over the destinies of this once great country." Conroy asked for an English peerage, the Ribbon of the Bath, and an annual pension of £3000. Victoria, apparently, gave her verbal consent to all this, probably to please her mother. But as soon as the Prime Minister heard of it, he canceled the pension and the admission to the Order of the Bath, and offered an Irish peerage— as Conroy was an Irishman—in place of an English one. Conroy refused, thus destroying his only chance of becoming a significant figure in the government of the new monarch.

The Victorian legend created

Victoria made her first appearance as Queen before the grandees of her court at half past eleven on the morning of the day of her accession. Lord Melbourne, the Prime Minister, led "the great assembly of lords and notables, bishops, generals, and Ministers of State" into the red saloon, where they laid eyes on their new Sovereign for the first time. These men "saw the doors thrown open and a very short, very slim girl in deep plain mourning come into the room alone and move forward to her seat with extraordinary dignity and grace; they saw a countenance, not beautiful, but prepossessing–fair hair, blue prominent eyes, a small curved nose, an open mouth revealing the upper teeth, a tiny chin, a clear complexion, and, over all, the strangely mingled signs of innocence, of gravity, of youth, and of composure; they heard a high unwavering voice reading aloud with perfect clarity; and then, the ceremony was over, they saw the small figure rise and, with the same consummate grace, the same amazing dignity, pass out from among them, as she had come in, alone."

Due to the fact that her mother and Conroy had kept Victoria as secluded as a nun in a convent her entire life, the new Queen was a figure of the greatest mystery to the men who would now be running her government. The Duchess of Kent and John Conroy were well known to them, but not the girl they had kept so assiduously under lock and key. They must have been filled with apprehension, considering all that they knew of her grandfather, father, and uncles. But the impression she created during this first brief audience at Kensington Palace was that of "astonishment and admiration". Conroy's appraisal of Victoria as "ignorant little child" was not entirely without foundation, though, if she was ignorant, he had no one to blame for that save himself, since he had been in charge of her education. But what Conroy failed to perceive, and the assembled councilors and ministers had grasped in an instant, was that even if Victoria had been deprived a thorough education in matters of state and government, she had nonetheless thought deeply about the fact that she was destined to be Queen, and imagination and study had bequeathed upon her a magisterial air, belying her age and gender.

Like most children with overly-controlling guardians, Victoria had watched people around her all her life for clues how to behave. She had met kings, queens, royal princes and princesses, and she had internalized their mannerisms. It would have been apparent to her from the time she was sixteen, if not earlier, that Conroy had no intention of preparing her for her future duties, which meant it was up to her to learn what she could, where she could. The result was that even if she *was* an ignorant child in many important ways, she did not strike her councilors and ministers as such; quite the opposite, in fact. In their eyes, "Her perceptions were quick, her decisions were sensible, her language was discreet; she performed her royal duties with extraordinary facility." Most striking of all was how different the new Queen seemed to be in comparison with the sons of King George III, "nasty old men, debauched and selfish, pig-headed and ridiculous, with their perpetual burden of debts, confusions, and disreputabilities." It seemed that, with the accession of this pretty, pink-cheeked, earnest young heiress, the Hanoverian blight "had vanished like the snows of winter, and here at last, crowned and radiant, was the spring."

Sir John Russell gave voice to these hopes in a welcoming oration before Parliament: "He hoped that Victoria might prove an Elizabeth without her tyranny, an Anne without her weakness. He asked England to pray that the illustrious Princess who had just ascended the throne with the purest intentions and the justest desires might see slavery abolished, crime diminished, and education improved. He trusted that her people would henceforward derive their strength, their conduct, and their loyalty from enlightened religious and moral principles, and that, so fortified, the reign of Victoria might prove celebrated to posterity and to all the nations of the earth."

Over the course of Victoria's reign—the longest of any monarch in English history until the Diamond Jubilee of Queen Elizabeth II in 2012—middle class British society would reorganize itself around the legend of Victoria as a moral leader, a model for the behavior of the nation. In this way, she was to redefine the British monarchy for centuries to come. And the seeds of her legend were planted in the first days of her reign, by the statesmen who saw a sheltered girl step forth from the shadows of the nursery, already in possession of herself and her authority, as though God had singled her out for her destiny. It was an image that, despite the occasional wobble, would be carefully cultivated for the next sixty-three years.

Influence

The banishment of John Conroy from Victoria's inner circle created a power vacuum around the sovereign which others hastened to fill. Our present concept of the English monarch is of a figurehead ruler who exerts little in the way of real political power, though in fact the present Queen possesses more governmental authority than most people are aware of. But in 1837, when Victoria succeeded to the throne, the monarch possessed a great deal of power indeed, and it was understood that she would exercise those powers on behalf of whoever succeeded in gaining her trust and confidence first. One person, and one person only from the household at Kensington continued to enjoy access to the Queen after she had relocated to the newly refurbished Buckingham Palace, and that was Victoria's beloved governess and Conroy's hated rival, Baroness Lehzen. Proximity to the head of state equals power, no matter what the system of government might be, and while Lehzen gave no indication that she was interested in influencing policy, there was very little separation between the personal and political in Victoria's life after she became Queen. Lehzen's influence mattered, all the more so after the Duchess of Kent

"...found herself, absolutely and irretrievably, shut off from every vestige of influence, of confidence, of power. She was surrounded, indeed, by all the outward signs of respect and consideration; but that only made the inward truth of her position the more intolerable. Through the mingled formalities of

Court etiquette and filial duty, she could never penetrate to Victoria. She was unable to conceal her disappointment and her rage. 'Il n'y a plus d'avenir pour moi,' she exclaimed to Madame de Lieven; 'je ne suis plus rien.' For eighteen years, she said, this child had been the sole object of her existence, of her thoughts, her hopes, and now—no! she would not be comforted, she had lost everything, she was to the last degree unhappy. Sailing, so gallantly and so pertinaciously, through the buffeting storms of life, the stately vessel, with sails still swelling and pennons flying, had put into harbour at last; to find there nothing—a land of bleak desolation."

Victoria's mother was relegated to a lavish suite of apartments in an entirely different part of the palace from the royal bedchambers; Baroness Lehzen, by contrast, slept in the bedroom next to the Queen's.

Two other persons enjoyed close proximity to the monarch immediately after her accession. One was Baron Stockmar, who served as an emissary for Victoria's uncle, King Leopold of Belgium. As the brother of the Duchess of Kent, Leopold had been given unusual access to Victoria when she was growing up. His letters to her had served as nearly the only tutelage she had ever received in international politics and affairs of state. Leopold was extremely anxious to retain his influence over his niece's thinking now that she occupied the throne. Baron Stockmar saw his own role in England not merely as an opportunity to further his sovereign's interest; he sincerely wished to be "the friend and adviser of a queen who was almost a child, and who, no doubt, would be much in need of advice and friendship."

Baroness Lehzen and Baron Stockmar remained close to Victoria throughout the early years of her reign, but even their influence over the young sovereign paled in comparison to the friendship that developed between the Queen and her Prime Minister, William Lamb, Lord Melbourne. He was of her father's party, for the Duke of Kent had grown increasingly involved in Whig politics after his marriage. It was Melbourne who would ultimately play the role in Victoria's life that John Conroy had intended for himself—that of father figure, confidante, conversational partner, tutor, and closest advisor.

Melbourne was an immensely talented yet complicated individual. His wife, the famous Lady Caroline Lamb, had conducted an infamous public affair with Lord Byron, just as Byron's poetry was achieving fame. The end of the affair had triggered a sort of mental breakdown in Lady Caroline, who died in an asylum, leaving Melbourne a handsome widower at the peak of his political career in his late forties. His only son had been born with some form of developmental delay or learning impairment, which had decided him against having any more children of his own, but he and his wife had become adoptive parents to a series of orphaned girls.

During the first three years of her reign, the relationship between the Queen and her Prime Minister came to resemble that of parent and adopted child, mentor and protégé, and even platonic lovers. Melbourne had a young and innocent mind to mold, and the Queen had a trusted elder figure with whom she could discuss all the business of her life—the personalities of the court, its scandals and upheavals. She had someone with whom she could exchange opinions about the music and literature she now had access to, along with all the other bright diversions that came flooding into her rapidly expanding world. It was Melbourne who arranged her coronation—a more modest affair than that arranged for George IV, but more suited to the majesty of a monarch than the perfunctory coronation of William IV.

One historian characterizes the relationship between Victoria and Melbourne thus:

"He became, in the twinkling of an eye, the intimate adviser and the daily companion of a young girl who had stepped all at once from a nursery to a throne... His behavior was from the first moment impeccable. His manner towards the young Queen mingled, with perfect facility, the watchfulness and the respect of a statesman and a courtier with the tender solicitude of a parent. He was at once reverential and affectionate, at once the servant and the guide. At the same time the habits of his life underwent a surprising change. His comfortable, unpunctual days became subject to the unaltering routine of a palace; no longer did he sprawl on sofas; not a single 'damn' escaped his lips. The man of the world who had been the friend of Byron and the regent... the cynic whose ribaldries had enlivened so many deep potations... might now be seen, evening after evening, talking with infinite politeness to a schoolgirl, bolt upright, amid the silence and the rigidity of Court etiquette. On her side, Victoria was instantaneously fascinated by Lord Melbourne... She found him perfect; and perfect in her sight he remained. Her absolute and unconcealed adoration was very natural; what innocent young creature could have resisted, in any circumstances, the charm and the devotion of such a man?"

The degree of intimacy that Victoria shared with Lord Melbourne would eventually expose her to gossip and speculations of the sort that royal courts throughout all of history seem to thrive on, particularly when the monarch is female and unmarried. But during the first three years of her reign, at least, Victoria was blissfully untroubled and unconcerned by any rumors, any wagging tongues, anything that might mar her happiness. She was Queen at last, and happier than she had ever been in her whole life.

The joyful Queen

At this stage in Victoria's life—immediately after her accession, before the duties of marriage, motherhood, and constitutional rule came to settle on her shoulders—she was predisposed to be delighted by everything. All her life she had been repressed, monitored, and controlled, and now all of a sudden every external restraint had been lifted. Any young person who found themselves suddenly in possession of a throne might have felt a similar euphoria, but Victoria's position was unique because she was a woman. In the early 19th century, young women from repressive families did not have many avenues of escape. The best they could hope for was to make a good marriage to a man they were fond of, who allowed them some personal freedom, and even then they would never entirely escape the family they had left behind. Only because she was Queen of England could Victoria do precisely as she liked. As a young Queen, Victoria in some ways brings to mind the heroine of Jane Austen's *Emma*, a novel which had so delighted George IV when he was Prince Regent that Austen had dedicated it to him. The fictional Emma Woodhouse, who "seemed to unite some of the best blessings of existence"—namely, money, health, cleverness, good looks, social position, and a simple, doting father who allowed her to do whatever she liked—enjoyed a degree of freedom rarely known to young women of her era, married or not. Of course, Victoria had an intrusive mother, rather than a doting father, but she possessed all the rest of Emma's blessings, and the fact that she was Queen meant that the annoying mother could be made quite irrelevant. From the ages of 18 to 21, Victoria was in a position to enjoy a unique degree of personal freedom virtually without restraint.

Furthermore, Victoria had one blessing Austen's heroine did not: she had meaningful work to do. As Queen, she had a realm to govern, daily reports from her ministers to read, state papers to peruse, correspondence from foreign monarchs to reply to. Her male predecessors had often found such work tedious, a distraction from the enjoyments of their royal privileges. But Victoria, whose opinions had scarcely ever been consulted even in matters pertaining to her own life, derived immense satisfaction from the fact that she was now *the* person to be consulted, the one person whose opinion mattered. The business of state was not a burden to her, but a vocation.

Added to all of this, she was now personally wealthy for the first time in her life. She had never suffered from want, of course, but her family had no money of its own, only allowances from Parliament, and Conroy had always controlled the income allotted to the Duchess of Kent's household. The allowance given to the monarch, however, numbered in six digits; it was, naturally, a princely sum in Victoria's eyes. The Kings before her had a penchant for exceeding these allowances, feeling that they had a right to run up as much debt as they liked. But Victoria's expenses were far more modest—her tastes, after all, did not run to gambling and drinking, nor did she have mistresses and illegitimate children to support. She therefore found it very easy to stay within the means allotted to her. She associated independence with remaining debt-free, so the first thing she did with her money was pay all of her father's debts in full. This was the beginning of a lifelong policy of frugality and decent business sense. Victoria made it her business as monarch to attend to the family finances, and by the end of her reign the royal family was wealthy in in its own right. By the time her children were grown, Parliamentary allowances were supplementary, rather than the main source of the royal income.

Politics and scandals

Victoria's reign began in June of 1837—"the pleasantest summer I EVER passed in MY LIFE, and I shall never forget this first summer of my reign," she wrote in her diary. But the next two years were not to remain so carefree. The inexperience and ignorance of which Conroy had spoken were to manifest themselves as the root of two major social and political scandals, which all but bankrupted the enormous stock of popularity and good will that Victoria inherited along with her crown.

Victoria's relationship with Lord Melbourne, her Prime Minister, ought to have provided her with the knowledge and perspective that would have helped her negotiate her way around these crises, but in many ways it had the opposite effect. Melbourne was fond of her—too fond, perhaps, too affectionate to play the role of a political mentor. And Victoria was dependent on Lord Melbourne to a degree that threatened constitutional entanglements.

The General Election of 1837 had greatly reduced the power of Melbourne's Whig government. Shifts in the balance of power in Parliament should have had little impact on the Queen; as a constitutional monarch, her official role was to consult and advise with the leaders of whichever party was in power, whether or not she agreed with their politics personally. But Melbourne was far more than Prime Minister to Victoria; he was the one person she depended upon personally above all others, almost as if he had been her husband or father. So even though her political beliefs were still raw and untutored, the declined of the Whig government was a source of extreme personal distress to the Queen, because if Lord Melbourne were no longer Prime Minister, it would mean an end to his frequent, almost daily visits to the palace. She expressed her dismay in her diary: "'I cannot say... how low, how sad I feel, when I think of the possibility of this excellent and truly kind man not remaining my Minister! Yet I trust fervently that He who has so wonderfully protected me through such manifold difficulties will not now desert me! I should have liked to have expressed to Lord M. my anxiety, but the tears were nearer than words throughout the time I saw him, and I felt I should have choked, had I attempted to say anything."

Victoria's partiality for Lord Melbourne concerned her ministers, who feared that she would be reluctant to extend equal cordiality to his Tory replacement when the time came. Sir Robert Peale was a very different sort of person from Melbourne; he was socially awkward and never seemed to know what to say to women in social settings. In her diary, Victoria relates an incident in which she had seen Peale "coming down the same street I was... the moment he saw me, he dashed down another street to avoid me, which I thought very rude." Melbourne, to his credit, assured the Queen that Peale had no intention of being rude; "That's his clumsiness," he explained. But Victoria, not yet much more than a clumsy child herself, could hardly be expected to bridge the social gap with this stranger who came to replace her beloved friend and mentor.

Victoria's political naiveté, and her inability to form a rapport with Robert Peale, gave rise to the so-called "Bedchamber Crisis" in 1839. That year, investigations into the brutal treatment of British slaves in Jamaica prompted Parliament to vote on a suspension of the Jamaican Constitution. The vote passed by a margin of only five votes, due to large numbers of former Whig supporters defecting across the aisle. Under these circumstances, Lord Melbourne felt obligated to resign as Prime Minister, which made it the Queen's responsibility to invite Tory party leaders to form a new government in her name. Accordingly, Victoria invited that legendary and redoubtable Tory, the Duke of Wellington, to become the new Prime Minister; but Wellington deferred to Robert Peale, who was much younger and had the better right, having been party leader during the last Tory government.

Victoria reluctantly invited Peale to the palace for an audience with the Queen, but the conversation, though cordial, led to a minor disaster. Both Victoria and Peale were nervous—Victoria, because of her age and inexperience, Peale because of his famous awkwardness, which was only exacerbated by his desire to make a good impression upon his new Queen. "You must remember that he is a man who is not accustomed to talk to Kings," Lord Melbourne explained to Victoria. "[He is] a man of quite different caliber; it's not like me; I've been brought up with Kings and princes which gives me that ease. I know the whole Family, and know exactly what to say to them; now he has not that ease and probably you were not at your ease."

Peale's inability to come to an understanding with the Queen arose from Victoria's ignorance regarding the vital yet unofficial role that society played in British politics at the time. There were essential components to how government functioned that were not covered in any textbooks on Constitutional law, having mostly to do with the role of women. In 1839, English women could not, of course, vote or hold office, but the wives, sisters, and daughters of politicians nonetheless possessed a considerable degree of unspoken power and wielded significant unofficial influence. It worked something like this: Whig politicians mingled in their free time with other Whig politicians, under the canny, watchful eyes of their wives, the eminent Whig hostesses, who presided over salons, dinners, balls, and hunts. These social occasions gave the men the opportunity to determine party platforms away from the listening ears of their opponents. Their female family members were responsible for creating these backroom channels of power; they also exercised their own powers by determining the guest lists (deciding who was "in" and who was "out"), making important introductions between established party leaders and up-and-coming members, and, of course, matchmaking between the young people to ensure the continuance of important Whig dynasties. The women also had their own means of influencing political agendas, sometimes by raising (or quashing) topics of conversation at the dinner table, sometimes by more direct means—during the height of the English abolition movement, for instance, hostesses made a point of not serving sugar with tea, since sugar came from the slave plantations in the East Indies.

Therefore, though the role of women in party politics was strictly unofficial, every canny, experienced British politician was aware that he ignored the ladies at his peril. This was as true in Tory circles as it was amongst Whig society. Melbourne and Robert Peale were both aware of it, but the unmarried, twenty-year-old Victoria was still more or less oblivious. She saw nothing inherently political in the fact that she socialized entirely in Whig circles, or in the fact that her friends were all persons who had been introduced to her by the Whig Prime Minister.

Melbourne was her most intimate friend, and therefore Melbourne's friends were her friends—the fact that they were all Whigs was beside the point.

When Victoria became Queen, it fell to her to appoint a select number of women as her Ladies of the Bedchamber—the traditional attendants who arranged the Queen's social calendar, looked after her wardrobe, and otherwise managed her affairs. Lacking a wide acquaintance in society, she naturally relied on Melbourne to suggest suitable candidates for these offices, and he, naturally, recommended women who were all wives of prominent Whig politicians. Since the marriage of her sister Feodore, Victoria had never had female friends her own age, so it was inevitable that she became very attached to her women. Again, she did not see the political message that such an arrangement was sending—she liked her attendants for their own sake, not because of their politics, or their husbands' positions. And this was where she clashed swords with Robert Peale. Having been asked by the Queen to form a government, Peale suggested that it would be difficult for him to do so while Her Majesty was attended exclusively by the wives and sisters of his political opponents. Might she, therefore, consider replacing a few of her Ladies of the Bedchamber with women from Tory families?

The request surprised and confused the young Queen. She did not understand that, as monarch, associating only with women from Whig families was tantamount to expressing a lack of faith and confidence in the Tory government. She understood only that she was being asked to part with her friends. Furthermore, she interpreted Peale's request as an attempt to test her limits— to discover if, on account of her age and sex, it would be possible for her ministers to bully and dictate to her in the future. It was a misunderstanding that Peale did not possess the social talents to clear up. Even Melbourne attempted to explain matters to her, assuring her that he could recommend suitable Tory ladies whose company she would find entirely congenial. But it was no use. Whatever Victoria lacked in astute political judgment she more than made up for with force of will. She refused Peale's request and congratulated herself on having demonstrated, like her uncle William IV, that she was Sovereign, no longer a child whose companions could be chosen and dismissed for her, as if by a governess.

The result was that Peale announced before Parliament that he could not form a government because he lacked the Queen's confidence; Lord Melbourne would have to continue as Prime Minister of a Whig government which did not possess the voting power it needed to pursue a legislative agenda. Victoria was delighted—she would not have to part with her friend Melbourne after all. Melbourne was more sensible to the damage that had been done, but he was likewise relieved that his daily intimacy with the Queen could continue. Outside of Buckingham Palace, however, the Bedchamber Crisis diminished the popularity and good will Victoria had enjoyed at the beginning of her reign. The sober, self-possessed, correct young woman who had appeared before her ministers on the morning of her accession seemed to have given way to a spoiled, ignorant person who could or would not understand where her duty lay. The Tories—historically, the party that supported the monarchy through fair weather and foul—began to perceive Victoria as the puppet of their political opponents, and withdraw their support.

Victoria's stubbornness was inherent to her nature, but it would be unfair to blame her for her political naiveté—that responsibility probably rests on Lord Melbourne's shoulders.

The Queen was young and did not know any better; Melbourne had spent hours in her company, gossiping and amusing himself, when he might have chosen to impart a stronger sense of where her duties lay. Victoria took every word that came from Melbourne's lips as gospel, so he would not have found her an inattentive pupil.

The Bedchamber Crisis damaged the confidence which Victoria's subjects placed in her, but an even greater crisis was shortly to come—one which, possibly, Melbourne might have helped her avoid, but whose roots lay deep in Victoria's troubled past at Kensington, and in her entrenched loathing for John Conroy.

Lady Flora Hastings

Almost from the moment of Victoria's accession, the Duchess of Kent ceased to be an intimate member of her inner circle—mother and daughter rarely saw or spoke to one another except at formal meal times, an exclusionary pattern which the Duchess resented deeply. This was due to two reasons; first, Victoria did not believe that her mother truly loved her, mostly because she had allowed Conroy so much control over her as a child. And second, Conroy was still on close terms with the Duchess. Victoria refused to see him, but he remained the comptroller of the Duchess's household, and there was nothing Victoria could do about it. The fact that her mother continued to rely upon a man Victoria hated so bitterly seemed only further proof that the Duchess's fondness for him eclipsed any affection or loyalty she felt for her daughter.

These domestic tensions were directly responsible for the second and far more severe scandal of Victoria's early reign: the affair of Lady Flora Hastings, who, more or less by accident, suffered the brunt of Victoria's frustrated desire to lash out against Conroy. Lady Flora Hastings, thirteen years Victoria's senior, was a friend of the Conroy family, and one of the "approved" companions Conroy had allowed Victoria to socialize with as a child. After the Kensington household moved to Buckingham Palace, Lady Flora accompanied the Duchess as her lady in waiting. She had a close relationship with John Conroy, and shared his antipathy towards Baroness Lehzen, who now ruled as the Queen's de facto private secretary. Since Victoria could not bear to hear a word spoken against Lehzen, and was suspicious of anyone close to Conroy, she considered Lady Flora fair game for petty gossip, making unkind remarks to

Melbourne about Lady Flora's appearance, which Melbourne did nothing to check.

Amongst Whig circles—which magnified the Queen's own prejudices many times beyond their initial scope—gossip about Lady Flora soon came to include damning insinuations about the nature of her relationship with Conroy. There were whispers that the married Conroy and Lady Flora were having an affair, baseless rumors that suddenly flourished into premium gossip when a prominent Whig hostess glimpsed Lady Flora riding in a carriage and noted that her waistline had expanded considerably. Lytton Strachey describes how the matter proceeded:

"Early in 1839, travelling in the suite of the Duchess, [Lady Flora] had returned from Scotland in the same carriage with Sir John. A change in her figure became the subject of an unseemly jest; tongues wagged; and the jest grew serious. It was whispered that Lady Flora was with child. The state of her health seemed to confirm the suspicion; she consulted Sir James Clark, the royal physician, and, after the consultation, Sir James let his tongue wag, too. On this, the scandal flared up sky-high. Everyone was talking; the Baroness was not surprised; the

Duchess rallied tumultuously to the support of her lady; the Queen was informed.

"At last the extraordinary expedient of a medical examination was resorted to, during which Sir James, according to Lady Flora, behaved with brutal rudeness, while a second doctor was extremely polite. Finally, both physicians signed a certificate entirely exculpating the lady. But this was by no means the end of the business. The Hastings family, socially a very powerful one, threw itself into the fray with all the fury of outraged pride and injured innocence; Lord Hastings insisted upon an audience of the Queen, wrote to the papers, and demanded the dismissal of Sir James Clark. The Queen expressed her regret to Lady Flora, but Sir James Clark was not dismissed. The tide of opinion turned violently against the Queen and her advisers; high society was disgusted by all this washing of dirty linen in Buckingham Palace; the public at large was indignant at the ill-treatment of Lady Flora. By the end of March, the popularity, so radiant and so abundant, with which the young Sovereign had begun her reign, had entirely disappeared."

This analysis of the incident, written in 1921, leaves certain details to the imagination that are less easily guessed at one hundred years later. The trouble was this: had Lady Flora and Conroy been conducting an affair, the Queen would have been within her rights to banish them both from the palace. But such a condemnation would ruin them both, Lady Flora in particular, so it would be unconscionable for Victoria to treat the rumors as fact unless she was moved by compelling evidence. There was no evidence, however, save that Lady Flora had undergone "a change in her figure" and consulted the palace doctor, Sir James Clark, who had insisted upon examining her naked. She had refused, and the doctor had told the Queen.

The wisest thing to do under the circumstances would have been for Victoria to simply wait the matter out; after all, a pregnancy only lasts for nine months at most. Instead, she permitted, even encouraged the gossip to such a degree that Lady Flora agreed to a medical examination to clear her name—that is, to certify that she was not pregnant. In the 1830's, pregnancy could not be determined with any certainty through an external examination unless fetal heartbeat was audible. Therefore, Lady Flora was forced to undergo a vaginal probe, which would determine whether the hymen was intact. Invasive medical procedures of this nature can be immensely upsetting to women even in this day and age. For an unmarried young woman of the early Victorian era, such a procedure, conducted twice, one by a "rude" doctor, was undoubtedly nothing short of traumatizing. When the doctors delivered their verdict that Lady Flora was a virgin and therefore could not be pregnant, her family, who were prominent Tories, were incensed—understandably so, especially considering that Sir James Clark had apparently not conducted his examination with the sort of delicacy the situation required. The Hastings wanted him dismissed; Victoria refused; the insult was compounded, and the Queen was seen as having grossly overstepped the bounds of decency in pursuit of a childhood grudge.

Only those closest to the Queen were aware that it was Conroy she had suspected of misconduct, far more than Lady Flora. Victoria's diaries from the Kensington period suggest that she had witnessed Conroy "taking liberties" of some sort with her mother, and she had indicated to Melbourne that she had witnessed such conduct from Conroy as would dispose her to believe him capable of anything. She did not like Lady Flora, but that was almost beside the point. Victoria had lost sight of the fact—or not yet fully realized—that as monarch, her least suggestion or whisper could result in disastrous consequences for the persons it concerned. To put it another way, she did not yet know her own strength. But this business was to teach her a hard lesson in monarchial privilege and its limits.

Not only was Lady Flora Hastings not pregnant, but the abdominal swelling which had altered her figure was actually due to a large, malignant tumor on her liver. For all his invasive examinations, Sir James Clark missed this entirely. Lady Flora would be dead of her malady by July of 1839, only a few months after the humiliating rumors had started. Naturally, she became a figure of intense sympathy and pity after her death, the innocent victim of a tale that cast the Queen in dreadful light. People began to whisper that Victoria was not so very different from her bad Hanoverian uncles after all. Confidence in Victoria's reign had begun to diminish during the Bedchamber Crisis, but the Flora Hastings affair completely eroded her early popularity. It was not a safe thing for a monarch to be unpopular at the dawn of the 1840s—it was a decade that would see popular rebellions sweeping almost all the major European nations, monarchs deposed, constitutions written, parliaments assembled. But Victoria was probably more chastised by the immediate social consequences her actions incurred. Aristocratic ladies hissed at the Queen when she appeared at

Ascot. Once, when she made a public appearance at the theater, an unknown lady in a nearby box shouted "Mrs. Melbourne" at her, loud enough for the entire audience to hear. The epithet which suggested that, in the eyes of some, Victoria's relationship with her Prime Minister was at least as suspicious as Lady Flora's friendship with John Conroy.

In short, 1839 was a disastrous year for the new Queen, and by the end of it, Victoria's closest advisors and family members had come to a conclusion. She was "dawdling"—putting off the serious duties of adulthood and monarchy in order to ride and dine and converse with her favorite, Melbourne. The conclusion was unanimous. If more crises like the Hastings affair were to be avoided, Victoria would have to settle properly into adult life. In other words, it was time for her to marry.

Prince Albert of Saxe-Coburg

If Victoria had little understanding of the delicate state of the European situation when she succeeded to the throne, it was due to a multitude of factors. Her youth was to blame, along with the glaring gaps in the education

Conroy had provided her, the failure of Lord Melbourne and others to supply those deficiencies once she was Queen—and then there was the fact that no one, on either side of the political aisle, was quite certain what role they needed or wanted the Queen to play in political affairs.

In the late 1830s, economic liberals in both parties were working for free trade and the abolition of tariffs on corn and wheat, which would drive down the price of bread for the poor and working classes. Liberals were also working to extend the franchise—that is, give voting rights to a greater number of Englishmen. They were opposed in endeavors by the conservative Tories, who, as members of the landed aristocracy, owned the land on which British wheat and corn were grown. A law that made imported grain cheaper would make it easier for the poor to feed themselves, but it would put a considerable dent in the wealth of the landowners whose income derived from the sale of domestic grain. And extending the vote would give a voice in the affairs of the nation to persons who were scarcely capable of understanding affairs of weight and moment—or so conservative thinking went.

Furthermore, Europe was reeling from the upsets of the Napoleonic era. The revolutionary fervor that began in America and France in the eighteenth century threatened to spread across the European continent in the wake of Napoleon's defeat. Nothing was more guaranteed to foment rebellion and anti-monarchist feeling among the common people like the perception that the ruling elite were indifferent to the hardships of the poor. No one in Parliament was certain what role the Queen should play in addressing these problems, but the scandals of 1839 weren't helping matters any—when the monarch was unpopular, the monarchy itself was unstable. No one wanted a domestic uprising on England's shores.

There was only one duty which everyone could agree fell unequivocally to the Sovereign. Now that Victoria was in her early twenties, it was imperative that she marry and produce an heir. The memory of George III and his fifteen children, who somehow managed to produce only one viable heir amongst them, was still fresh in everyone's minds. Even in a constitutional monarchy, it was vital to the stability of the nation for the line of the royal succession to be settled and secure. The sooner Victoria chose a suitable husband and began having children, the better off everyone would be. However, there were a limited number of suitable matrimonial candidates for the Queen to choose from. Most of the royalty of Europe were Catholic. But anti-Catholic sentiments in England were at a high tide; Roman Catholic emancipation had only come to England ten years previously, and the fight to extend the franchise to Catholics had faced bitter opposition. Rebellion might very well ensue if Victoria were to marry a Hapsburg, or a Bourbon.

It was clear that the Queen must marry a Protestant, but this confined her options to the House of Orange, the House of Coburg, or one of her own English cousins. William IV had been in favor of a Dutch marriage, but Victoria had already judged Prince Alexander a lumpen bore. Her cousin George of Cambridge, on the other hand, was not quite respectable, at least in Victoria's opinion. (Cambridge, perhaps feeling that the grapes he had been denied were a bit sour, later commented that he could never have married his dumpy little cousin in any case.) This left her Coburg cousins, Ernest and Albert, whose visit to Kensington four years previously had been such a success. Lord Melbourne did not approve of a Coburg match; he disliked Germans in general, and the Duke of Coburg, Ernest and Albert's father, was not well thought of; he had divorced his wife, the Duchess Luise, and the Coburg family in general were notorious for spawning illegitimate children and contracting venereal diseases.

But what did Victoria think? The Duchess of Kent had wanted her to marry Ernest, but it was Albert who had drawn Victoria's eye four years ago. Did she prefer Albert still? Compared to his brother, yes, but that was irrelevant—Victoria did not *wish* to marry. Why should she? Certainly, she understood that it would be a disaster for the nation if she were to die and the throne were to pass to her uncle, the Duke of Cumber and King of Hanover. But she was only twenty years old; there would be plenty of time to choose a husband and produce an heir in three, four, five years' time. A husband would only threaten her independence; for everything that was charming about male companionship, she could rely on Lord Melbourne. So long as she remained Sovereign and Melbourne remained her friend, she could not imagine being happier than she already was—"any change would be for the worse", she felt, *especially* marriage.

"What was tiresome," write one chronicler of the period, "was that her uncle Leopold had apparently determined, not only that she ought to marry, but that her cousin Albert ought to be her husband... it was true that long ago, in far-off days, before her accession even, she had written to him in a way which might well have encouraged him in such a notion. She had told him then that Albert possessed 'every quality that could be desired to render her perfectly happy,' and had begged her 'dearest uncle to take care of the health of one, now so dear to me, and to take him under your special protection,' adding, 'I hope and trust all will go on prosperously and well on this subject of so much importance to me.' Victoria worried that she had expressed herself too freely and that her words were now being construed as a kind of promise. Albert had undoubtedly been a delightful novelty during the days when she was a virtual prisoner at Kensington, but she had been younger then, starved of any other amusements. Nowadays, thoughts of Albert scarcely crossed her mind.

All of that changed, however, in the autumn of 1839, when Victoria's uncle Leopold arranged for Albert and his brother Ernest to make a second visit to England. Victoria, of course, knew precisely what her uncle intended by this; her only doubt was whether Albert was "aware of the wish of his Father...relative to me". As recently as April of 1839 Victoria had told Lord Melbourne that "at present, my feeling is quite against ever marrying." She wrote to King Leopold, stressing that while she was happy to welcome her cousins when they came to visit, she had not and would not make any promises.

For Albert's part, he was very much aware that Victoria had no fixed intention of marrying him, and he somewhat resented being trotted out for a second inspection. But it was just as well that he agreed to the visit anyway, because Victoria's feelings changed dramatically once she had seen Albert face to face again. When the Coburg brothers appeared in England on October 10, 1839, "the whole structure of [Victoria's] existence crumbled into nothingness like a house of cards." Albert was extraordinarily good looking—at least by the standards of the time. A mere four days in his company, dancing, riding horses, and conversing, were enough to prompt Victoria's change of heart. Shyly, she informed Lord Melbourne that her feelings about marriage were now very different than what they had been only a few weeks earlier. Melbourne acknowledged the transformation with a light comment and changed the subject. He knew, of course, that her marriage was inevitable, but it was a subject that could only bring pain to him. Once she had selected a husband, the greater part of their friendship would dwindle away to fond but formal interactions, only in public, never again in private.

On the fifth day of Albert's visit, Victoria asked to speak with him privately. The subject had to be approached with some delicacy, for Victoria's position was unusual, even unique. It was scarcely the custom for young ladies in the 19th century to propose marriage to the man they preferred, but Victoria had no other choice—she was the Queen, and no man could propose to *her*.

Victoria's diary contains an account of the conversation, and it is clear that she chose her words very carefully: "...After a few minutes I said to him that I thought he must be aware why I wished them to come here—and that it would make me too happy if he would consent to what I wished (to marry me.)" The words in parentheses would have gone unspoken out of feminine delicacy, but the words "consent to what I wished" would have left Albert in no doubt of what she was trying to say. His response was positive; they "embraced each other, and he was so kind, so affectionate." She said that she was quite unworthy of him, while he murmured that he would be very happy..." When the conversation was over, she wrote that felt herself to be "the happiest of human beings."

Others were not so happy. The general public were delighted by the prospect of a royal marriage, but her English relations were affronted that she had married a German—they considered it the doing of her German mother, who had kept Victoria so isolated from the English side of her family while she was growing up. And then there was Lord Melbourne, whose opinion had always meant to much to Victoria. He recognized the necessity, the inevitability of her marrying, and he had nothing against Albert personal, save that he was a German. But Melbourne's relationship with Victoria contained elements of infatuation. Theirs was a kind of platonic romance with no hope of consummation. The friendship they had enjoyed—familiar, full of jokes, almost entirely informal—could not in propriety continue after her engagement.

In 1841, when the Whigs fell out of power, Melbourne's term as Prime Minister came to an end, and with it his daily access to the Queen. She wished to continue writing to him, but it was pointed out to her that it looked very bad from a political point of view for a monarch to continue on terms of such intimacy with a politician who was no longer head of her government. For Victoria, who had all the delights of a happy marriage and, soon, motherhood to distract her, the loss of Melbourne's company was bittersweet. But for Lord Melbourne himself, it was akin to a tragedy, for his feelings for Victoria were a muddle of fatherly affection and romantic devotion. Though he stepped aside with good grace when the time came, he felt the loss of their relationship so keenly that it became unbearably painful to him even to drive past Buckingham Palace. Victoria offered him an earldom in compensation for his services to the Crown, but Melbourne refused this honor, asking instead for some lithographs—an early form of photograph—bearing her image. The loss of his political standing was nothing to him; the loss of the young Queen's friendship was everything.

Chapter Three: Victoria and Albert (1840-1861)

"This pair of extremely strong characters was in for an extraordinary journey together when they married. Both wanted power. Neither wanted to surrender their independence. More than in most marriages there was a thunderous clash of wills. There was also, however, a deep bond from the very first. Furious as they would be with one another in the first stormy two years, as they were also in the tired last year, they remained everlastingly a team."

A.N. Wilson, *Victoria: A Life*

A legendary marriage

It was traditional for royal marriages to take place at night, but Victoria and Albert were married on a gusty, rainy afternoon at 1 pm on February 10, 1840, at the Chapel Royal at St James's. Victoria's wedding gown, and that of the bridesmaids carrying her train, was white, and this set the fashion for white satin wedding dresses which has endured to the present day. (Previously, a bride would be married in her best dress, of whatever color and material were available.)

There had been some inconveniences before the wedding regarding Albert's official status. First, there was the matter of his income—as a member of the immediate royal family he was entitled to an allowance, the exact amount of which was to be set by Parliament. Lord Melbourne suggested that Albert be given the same amount which had been granted to King Leopold when he was married to Princess Charlotte. The Tories rallied in opposition against him, however, and the allowance was set at £31,000—Leopold had received £50,000. Then there was the matter of his title. When a reigning king married, his wife became Queen Consort more or less by default, but when a reigning queen took a husband, he was eligible for the title of either King Consort or Prince Consort. Constitutionally, there was no difference between the two titles; the duties of a King Consort were the same as those of the Prince Consort, that is, to support and uphold the authority of the Queen. But for some reason—perhaps because people had enough difficulty wrapping their heads around the idea of a woman having higher status than her husband without making their titles sound too much alike—King Consort was a title rarely used in England. In this case, Victoria wanted Albert to be named King, but Lord Melbourne persuaded her against it.

Melbourne's Whig government had, however, attempted to insert Albert into the line of English succession; that is, should Victoria die before producing an heir of her own body, Albert would succeed her as King of England. There was some precedent for monarchs being succeeded by their spouses—in the 18th century, Peter the Great of Russia had named his wife, a peasant by birth, to succeed him as Empress—but it was not at all the normal way of things. Melbourne's suggestion was not well received by the remaining descendants of George III, who were not prepared to sit idly by while they were cut out of the line of succession by a foreigner.

All the inconveniences aside, the marriage itself was a pleasant affair for the couple themselves. Victoria anticipated the wedding night with all the raptures of a young woman in love and all the nervousness of a young woman of the early 19th century who had not been well-prepared for the realities of sexual intercourse, but had heard enough to make her extremely nervous:

"We had our dinner in our sitting room; but I had such a sick headache that I could eat nothing, and was obliged to lie down in the middle blue room for the remainder of the evening on the sofa; but, ill or not, I never, never spent such an evening!! My dearest dearest dear Albert sat on a footstool at my side, and his excessive love and affection gave me feelings of heavenly love and happiness, I never could have hoped to have felt before! He clasped me in his arms, and we kissed each other again and again! His beauty, his sweetness and gentleness—really, how can I ever be thankful enough to have such a Husband! At half past ten I went and undressed and was very sick, and at 20 minutes past ten we both went to bed; (of course in one bed), to lie by his side and in his arms, and on his dear bosom, and be called by name of tenderness, I have never yet heard used to me before—was bliss beyond belief! Oh! This was the happiest day of my life!"

We must suppose that Albert was exerting himself to be generous and kind to his new bride on their wedding night, because there was much about his new situation that did not please him. It was difficult, for instance, for him to be in a foreign country, surrounded by Englishmen, far away from his family and friends. He was even forbidden by Lord Melbourne to bring his own German private secretary from home to keep him company; an Englishman had already been selected for the job, and Albert had no choice but to accept him, though he made a point of informing the luckless person that he was by no means Albert's first choice for the job.

It is scarcely surprising that Albert should find himself homesick and at a loss after accepting the Queen's proposal of marriage. The change in his position necessarily resulted in a complete upset of all his private affairs. What is somewhat more surprising is the assertion of one historian that Albert, destined to become one half of the most famous marriage in English history, "was not in love with [Victoria]"—at least, not when he accepted her proposal of marriage. Rather, it was the position itself which attracted him, and the opportunity to exercise royal influence and authority. This historian writes:

"Affection, gratitude, the natural reactions to the unqualified devotion of a lively young cousin who was also a queen–such feelings possessed him, but the ardours of reciprocal passion were not his. Though he found that he liked Victoria very much, what immediately interested him in his curious position was less her than himself. Dazzled and delighted, riding, dancing, singing, laughing, amid the splendours of Windsor, he was aware of a new sensation–the stirrings of ambition in his breast. His place would indeed be a high, an enviable one! And then, on the instant, came another thought. The teaching of religion, the admonitions of Stockmar, his own inmost convictions, all spoke with the same utterance. He would not be there to please himself, but for a very different purpose–to do good. He must be 'noble, manly, and princely in all things,' he would have 'to live and to sacrifice himself for the benefit of his new country;' to 'use his powers and endeavours for a great object–that of promoting the welfare of multitudes of his fellowmen.' One serious thought led on to another. The wealth and the bustle of the English Court might be delightful for the moment, but, after all, it was Coburg that had his heart. 'While I shall be untiring,' he wrote to his grandmother, 'in my efforts and labours for the country to which I shall in future belong, and where I am called to so high a position, I shall never cease ein treuer Deutscher, Coburger, Gothaner zu sein.'"

If it is indeed the case that Albert was less in love with Victoria than she with him as of 1840, he never gave her reason to suspect it. But as to the other matter—his desire to exercise authority through his wife—Victoria was quickly conscious of it, and troubled by it, for she had not married him with any intention of giving up any of her power. In the weeks leading up to her marriage, she became so ill that her doctor was certain she was developing a case of measles. But it was not measles; it was anxiety. Fear of what was to come after the marriage—not just the mysterious duties of the marital bed, but the well-known vows of the marriage ceremony, in which she would have to pledge to honor and obey another person, just as she had been compelled to honor and obey the Duchess of Kent and Sir John Conroy for so many unhappy years in her childhood—made her so ill that she was forced her to take to her bed. "No doubt," writes the same historian, "she loved Albert; but she loved power too." But she had one consolation at least, for "one thing was certain: she might be Albert's wife, but she would always be Queen of England."

The making of a consort

When one studies the lives of the queens and empresses of Europe in past centuries, one begins to perceive a common thread: the delight of the new queen in her newfound authority and independence, followed swiftly by the fear that these joys will be taken away from her if and when she marries. Likewise, when one studies the lives of the men who marry or become the "favorites" of queens and empresses, another common set of tropes begins to emerge: the raptures of the honeymoon swiftly giving way to disappointment and listlessness, as the newlywed prince discovers that he has no place, no purpose, no function that is not ornamental. Ambition and the desire for power motivated him to marry a supremely powerful woman, but that ambition now turns to stagnation and restlessness, as it begins to dawn on him that he will always be second in power and importance to his wife. He begins to compare himself to his male friends; they may lack a consort's crown, but at least they are masters in their own home. Not so him; a virtual independent organization of staff and servants exist to run the household for him, and any interference on his part is decidedly unwelcome.

Monarchy falls to men far more often than it falls to women, and queens consort usually find their duties cut out for them: they become mothers, hostesses, diplomats, and emissaries of royal benevolence to the nation. In marrying a king, a queen consort ascends to the peak of female authority; her duties are, in a sense, no different from any woman, only carried out on a grander scale. But just as Victoria, and the queens regnant who preceded her, essentially stepped into a male role upon their succession, the only role ever marked out for the spouse of a consort were duties that no 19th century male could take upon himself without sacrificing that ephemeral quality known as "manliness", which is so often tied into self-respect and self-worth. Adelaide, wife of William IV, was supposed to find contentment and meaning in supporting her husband and making his royal household comfortable. Albert, husband of Victoria, was supposed to find his duty in supporting his wife and helping her to produce a royal heir. Beyond that, no one really knew what to do with him. He wanted and desired an active role in politics and government, but there was no Constitutional provision for this. If he wanted to be Victoria's co-ruler, he had to persuade Victoria to share power with him.

Victoria's greatest strength—which was also, at times, a weakness—was her resistance to persuasion and influence. She was not prepared to surrender or share any of her authority, at least not at first. To do so, she feared, would be to return to the miseries of her early childhood, when Conroy and her mother decided everything for her. She had every confidence that Albert would be a perfect husband, but she did not want him to be more. At one point early in their engagement there was a proposal that Albert be given an English peerage, which would entitle him to a seat in the House of Lords. Victoria had explained to Albert that Parliament was not likely to approve the proposal. "The English," she explained, "are very jealous of any foreigner interfering in the government of this country, and have already in some of the papers expressed a hope that you would not interfere. Now, though I know you never would, still, if you were a Peer, they would all say, the Prince meant to play a political part. I know you never would!"

But he wanted to, and deep down, Victoria knew it. So did Lord Melbourne, who confided to George Anson, Albert's private secretary, that "the prince is indolent, and it would be better if he was more so, for in his position we want no activity." Anson, though new to his role, must have already begun to feel loyalty towards Albert, for he replied that, "the prince may be indolent, but it results from there being no scope for his energy. If you required a Cipher in the difficult position of Consort of the Queen you ought not to have selected the prince. Having got him, you must make the most of him. When he [sees] the power of being useful to the Queen he will act."

Lord Melbourne and Baroness Lehzen were the real obstacles standing in Albert's way. Lord Melbourne was, in effect, the Queen's private secretary—a conflict of interest, perhaps, for the Prime Minister, but beyond rectifying, so long as Victoria was seeing him daily. And Baroness Lehzen managed everything to do with the Queen's domestic life—Albert could not be master of his own home while Lehzen reigned. Albert himself had only one devoted ally, and that was Baron Stockmar, formerly the emissary of Leopold of Belgium. It was Stockmar who set out to cultivate Albert and make him into something more than a figurehead prince.

Stockmar's task—taking Albert in hand—was not easy in the beginning. Albert was suffering from a kind of depression. His duties, such as they were, bored him, and as to expanding his role into something more meaningful, it was apparent to him that no one besides Baron Stockmar wished him to do it. But Stockmar was relentless: "Incessantly, he harped upon two strings—Albert's sense of duty and his personal pride. Had the Prince forgotten the noble aims to which his life was to be devoted? And was he going to allow himself, his wife, his family, his whole existence, to be governed by Baroness Lehzen?" The problem, as Albert and Stockmar both saw it, was that the Baroness "encouraged the Queen to have secrets". Victoria, they believed, was naturally honest to a fault, too artless to "manage" Albert in the way she was doing (that is, steering every conversation they had away from politics) unless Lehzen was coaching her.

Was Victoria being managed herself by a former governess who wished to retain her influence over the queen even when it would be more natural for Victoria to consult her husband? Or had Victoria confided to the Baroness that Albert, against her wishes, was angling for power, and taken her advice on how to deftly change the subject whenever political topics arose? Lytton Strachey's analysis, written in 1921, contains such blatant patriarchal bias that it is difficult to guess at the truth. For instance, Strachey asserts that Albert was, "he knew very well, his wife's intellectual superior"—an assertion which he does not support with any evidence—"and yet [Albert] found, to his intense annoyance, that there were parts of her mind over which he exercised no influence. When, urged on by the Baron, he attempted to discuss politics with Victoria, she eluded the subject, drifted into generalities, and then began to talk of something else." Stockmar blamed this evasiveness on Lehzen, but from a more contemporary perspective, Victoria's tendency to "[elude] the subject" and "[drift] into generalities" sounds like the skilled social training of an aristocratic young woman using conversational gambits to avoid open conflict with a husband who is attempting to trespass on her role as head of state. As to there being "parts of her mind" that Albert could not influence, it is difficult to imagine any person who would be willing to subject the entirety of their thinking to another person's influence.

When Albert did begin to take a more active role in politics, it was due to two factors: the retirement of Lord Melbourne in 1841, and the birth of his and Victoria's first six children—all of whom were born between 1840 and 1848. Melbourne had been acting as the Queen's de facto private secretary since her accession, a position of immense responsibility, as the private secretary set the tone for the monarch's interactions with Parliament and was largely responsible for defining the role of the monarchy itself. This was the position the Sir John Conroy had wanted for himself when Victoria was younger. Victoria was almost constantly pregnant or recovering from childbirth for most of the 1840s (with three more children to come between 1850 and 1857), so when Melbourne stepped down, she was forced to rely on others. This gave Albert the opportunity to set his own political agenda, which aimed to elevate the monarchy above party politics altogether. Victoria had been a proud Whig all her life, but

Albert disdained both Whigs and Tories. "The Whigs seek to change before change is required," he wrote in his private journals. "The love of change is their great failing. The Tories on the other hand resist change long after the feeling and temper of the times has loudly demanded it and at last make a virtue of necessity by ungracious concession. My endeavor will be to form my opinions quite apart from politics and party, and I believe such attempt may succeed."

It was perhaps a noble sentiment, but inherently naïve, no more grounded in reality than Victoria's refusal to dismiss her Whig ladies during the Bedchamber Crisis. The monarchy itself was anything but apolitical—it had always been supported by the most conservative elements in Parliament. That said, from a public relations standpoint, Albert's determination that "the Crown should be above politics" would come to define how the monarchy was perceived by the British people. Even today, the Queen is conceived of as a figurehead, serving no particular political agenda. Albert's vision, naïve or not, probably played a major role in preserving England from the wave of popular revolutions that swept every other major European nation during the 1840s, thus enabling the monarchy as an institution to survive into the present day.

Family life

The fact that Victoria, in the midst of ruling a country, managed to bear nine children in seventeen years, losing not one of her offspring to death in infancy nor succumbing herself to puerperal fever, hemorrhaging, or toxemia, was a feat of extraordinary physical stamina and tremendous good luck, since little credit can be given to her doctors in an age when medical science still relied on treatments such as blisters and bloodletting to treat all manner of illnesses. By the end of Victoria's reign in the 1890s, the infant mortality rate in England was 150 deaths for every 1000 live births, and the maternal mortality was correspondingly high. By contrast, the size and health of Victoria's family was nothing less than a miracle of fecundity, especially considering the paucity of heirs produced by the rest of George III's descendants. The great English kings of old had won renown for their feats of physical bravery on the battlefield; a Queen undertook no lesser a degree of physical risk by undergoing the perils of the childbed, but that sort of courage and strength seemed to impress people less. However, Victoria's procreative feats had as enduring an impact on the future of European politics as Napoleon's attempt to conquer the continent in the decades previous.

As historian A.N. Wilson, puts its, "The strength of [Victoria and Albert's] personal attraction, and the Queen's physical stamina, led to the birth of nine children, all of whom survived birth and childhood. This was in itself something of an achievement in the nineteenth century. It was also a political statement. Their private life was not really a private life, however much they might wish it to be so. For each coition was not only an act of love, but a gesture against the swell of European republicanism. Each pregnancy brought forth a potential German empress, the would-be parent of a Russian tsar, the potential for a queen of Spain or a tsar of Bulgaria."

Victoria's first-born child was, to the disappointment of both parents, a daughter: Victoria, the Princess Royal, born on November 21, 1840, about eight months after her parents' marriage. Her destiny was to become Queen of Prussia and Empress of Bismarck's newly-unified Germany. At the age of 18, Princess Victoria married Frederick, son of Kaiser Wilhelm I. Frederick was suffering from the end stages of cancer by the time of his accession and reigned for only two months, but their son, Kaiser Wilhelm II, had a far more measurable impact on European politics. His close family relationship to the British royals produced a lifelong obsession with the British navy and a corresponding sense of rivalry that led directly to the outbreak of the first World War.

Victoria's second child, born November 9, 1841, almost exactly a year after his sister, was Albert, Prince of Wales, who succeeded Victoria on her death as King Edward VII of England. The third child, Princess Alice, was born on April 25, 1843. At the age of 19, Alice married Louis VI, Grand Duke of Hesse. They had seven children, one of whom, Princess Alix, married Tsar Nicholas II of Russia and became known as Empress Alexandra. She was effectively, and for a time, officially, co-ruler of Russia. Her eccentric, myopic attitude towards the turbulent unrest in turn-of-the-century Russia played a large role in provoking the revolution of 1917.

The fourth child of Victoria and Albert, Prince Alfred, Duke of Edinburgh, was born August 6, 1844. When he was thirty, he married the Grand Duchess Maria Alexandrovna, daughter of Tsar Alexander II of Russia; their daughter Marie would become Queen of Romania.

The younger children—Princess Helena, born in 1846, Princess Louise, born in 1848, Prince Arthur, born in 1850, Prince Leopold, born 1853, and Princess Beatrice, born 1857, made less illustrious marriages than their elder siblings, but they still made their genetic mark on history. Victoria Eugenie, daughter of Princess Beatrice and Prince Henry of Battenberg, became Queen of Spain. More importantly, by dispatching their children in marriage to Russia, Germany, Spain, Schleswig-Holstein, and elsewhere across Europe, Victoria established a network of alliances that essentially converted all the monarchies of Europe into one large extended family. The "ignorant little child" who had inherited a throne at eighteen would have a more measurable effect on the politics of Europe than any of her forebears, male or female, or any of her descendants. She defined monarchy during the last era of history in which monarchy was the default form of government.

But motherhood did not come easily or naturally to Victoria at first. Her pregnancies were often difficult, and she sometimes suffered from post-partum depression. In her diaries, she refers to having "the first two years of my married life utterly spoiled by this occupation"—meaning pregnancy and childbirth. She became short-tempered and often fought with Albert during these early years, not over politics, but over the ordinary domestic arrangements of their expanding household. Albert despised Victoria's physician, the same James Clark who had so offended Lady Flora Hastings, and he felt obliged to demand the removal of Baroness Lehzen, who exerted absolute authority over the royal nursery. Albert wrote to Baron Stockmar that he considered Lehzen "a crazy, stupid intriguer, obsessed with the lust of power, who regards herself as a demi-God, and anyone who refuses to recognize her as such is a criminal." He had complained before of Lehzen's interfering in his marriage, but after the birth of their first children, her character apparently underwent a change for the worse. "I declare to you," Albert wrote to Stockmar, "as my and Victoria's true friend, that I will sacrifice my own comfort, my life's happiness to Victoria in silence, even if she continues in her error. But the welfare of my children and Victoria's existence as sovereign are too sacred for me not to die fighting rather than yield them as prey to Lehzen."

Finally, in 1841, around the same time that Lord Melbourne began to fade away from the royal couple's lives, the Queen reluctantly sent Lehzen back to Germany, where she remained for the rest of her life. Domestic harmony at the palace improved greatly after her removal. Even the Duchess of Kent was restored to the family fold— Albert believed that a reconciliation between mother and daughter would have taken place years before had it not been for Baroness Lehzen continuing to remind Victoria of the old grudge between them. Once Lehzen was gone, he began drawing his mother in law back into the family circle, where she doted on her new grandchildren. It was a new era in Victoria's life—looking back on old entries in her diary, finding passages in which she had expressed the feeling that she could never be happier than she was as a young unmarried Queen continually in the company of Lord Melbourne, she added a note from the the present: "Reading this again, I cannot forbear remarking what an artificial sort of happiness MINE was THEN, and what a blessing it is I have now in my beloved Husband REAL and solid happiness, which no Politics, no worldly reverses CAN change; it could not have lasted long as it was then, for after all, kind and excellent as Lord M. is, and kind as he was to me, it was but in Society that I had amusement, and I was only living on that superficial resource, which I THEN FANCIED was happiness! Thank God! for ME and others, this is changed, and I KNOW WHAT REAL HAPPINESS IS–V. R."

Assassination attempts

As far the Queen's relationship with her subjects, which had suffered so much during the Bedchamber Crisis and the affair of Lady Flora Hastings, the popularity and good will she had inadvertently squandered were revived by a most unexpected means: people kept trying to assassinate her. In fact, Victoria would be the target of at least seven assassination attempts throughout her reign, five of them occurring between 1840 and 1850.

The first assassination attempt occurred on June 10, 1840, when Victoria was in the early stages of her first pregnancy. At six in the evening, the royal phaeton had set out from Buckingham Palace, carrying Victoria and Albert to visit the Duchess of Kent, who by now had her own independent establishment a short distance from the palace. As the vehicle rounded a corner, two shots from two guns were fired at the Queen's phaeton. This was more than a century before security measures surrounding public figures had developed into the precise science it is today; European monarchs staged guards at the entrances to their palaces to keep potential angry mobs from battering down the gates, but they did not, as a rule, travel with personal guards when they went out in public. Even if they had taken such a precaution, royal guards were soldiers, trained to fight in open combat, not to prevent the actions of a single gunman who cared little if he happened to be caught. The shots went awry and no one was harmed, but the baffled driver made the mistake of stopping the coach in its tracks before an irritable Albert commanded him to drive on. Bystanders, who had come to watch the Queen drive past, rushed towards the shooter and held him until two police officers arrived to take him into custody. His name was Edward Oxford, an unemployed former tavern worker. He made no attempt to hide his guilt: "It is I, it was me that did it," he proclaimed, as the police seized him.

Oxford was charged and tried, but the police were unable to find any discharged ammunition from the shooting. Oxford's attorneys therefore made the case that the two pistols he was carrying had been loaded with powder but not with shot, and thus he could not be considered guilty of treason, since there was no possibility of his actions harming the Queen. He was ultimately found insane and confined in a mental asylum for an indefinite term. No motive was ever found, but his mother testified that he had been behaving oddly for weeks before the shooting. When his room was searched, police found a pamphlet for a nonexistent political society that required its members to be armed with a brace of pistols and other weapons at all times. If Oxford had been acting as part of a conspiracy, it was a conspiracy that existed only in his head.

The British people were deeply impressed by the physical courage and cool head displayed by the Queen in the face of this and subsequent attacks. She herself was unimpressed by Oxford's insanity conviction; in her opinion, he knew precisely what he was doing. The 1840s was a decade for assassinations in Britain; a year later, another gunman attempted to assassinate the Prime Minister, Sir Robert Peale, but mistakenly shot and killed his secretary instead. By this time, Victoria had an excellent relationship with Peale and considered him a friend, so the murder upset her greatly. Many years and several more assassination attempts later, in 1882, she wrote to her then Prime Minister, Lord Gladstone, complaining of the lenient sentencing these would-be assassins had received:

"Punishment deters not only sane men but also eccentric men, whose supposed involuntary acts are really produced by a diseased brain capable of being acted upon by external influence. A knowledge that they would be protected by an acquittal on the grounds of insanity will encourage these men to commit desperate acts, while on the other hand certainty that they will not escape punishment will terrify them into a peaceful attitude towards others."

In other words, she believed that had Edward Oxford met with a sterner punishment for his crime in 1840, it might have deterred some of his followers—such as John Francis and John William Bean, both of whom shot at the Queen in the summer of 1842. As with the Oxford shooting, both of these assassination attempts took place while Victoria and Albert were leaving the grounds of Buckingham Palace in an open carriage. In the case of John Francis, a police constable saw him take him aim at the Queen and rushed at him before he could fire. The pistol was discharged in the scuffle, but no one was hurt. The Sheffield Independent newspaper reported on the case:

"JOHN FRANCIS was placed at the bar, charged on the indictment that he being a subject of our Lady the Queen, and not regarding the duty of his allegiance, as a false traitor against our said Lady the Queen, on the 30th May, 1842, at Westminster, did shoot off and discharge a certain pistol loaded with gunpowder and a bullet, which he in his right hand held at and against the person of our said Lady the Queen, with intent thereby and therewith maliciously and traitorously to shoot, assassinate, kill, and put to death our said Lady the Queen ; and thereby had traitorously and maliciously made a direct attempt against the life of our said Lady the Queen. The second overt act varied only from the first by stating that the pistol was loaded with gunpowder and certain other destructive materials and substances to the persons unknown. The third overt act charged was the same, only for shooting off and discharging a certain loaded pistol. The fourth was the same, only for shooting and discharging a certain pistol."

Francis was ultimately convicted and sentenced to death by hanging, but the Queen chose to commute his sentence to transportation— meaning that he was sent to Australia, that famous 19th century dumping-ground for English criminals. Bizarrely, sixteen-year old John William Bean, who shot at Victoria and Albert one month later, claimed that, like Oxford, he had not loaded his pistols with anything but powder and wadding paper. He didn't want to hurt the Queen, he explained; he only wanted to be sent to Australia at the Crown's expense, so he could start a new life. Instead, he was convicted of misdemeanor assault and sentenced to a term of 18 months at Newgate prison.

One would think that Victoria might have begun to reconsider her habit of riding in open carriages, especially after she was shot at yet again in May of 1849, at the exact same hour and location where Edward Oxford shot at her nine years before. This time, however, she was alone. The gunman was an Irishman named William Hamilton. The Manchester Courier reported Hamilton's trial:

"Upon the learned judges taking their seats upon the bench, the prisoner William Hamilton was placed at the bar, to plead to the indictment charging him with a misdemeanor, having unlawfully discharged a pistol at her Majesty. The indictment alleged that the prisoner, on the 19th day of May, at the parish of St. Martin-in-the-Fields, having in his possession a certain pistol loaded with an explosive substance—to wit, gunpowder—unlawfully, willfully, and maliciously discharged the said pistol at her Majesty, with intent thereby to injury to her person. In other counts of the indictment the intent the prisoner was laid to be to alarm her Majesty, and to cause a breach of the peace."

It was almost as if firing upon the Queen had become something of a rite of passage for impoverished malcontents with troubled pasts, and so long as no blood was shed, was no longer considered a serious enough crime to warrant a treason charge. Hamilton was sentenced to transportation and sent to Australia. By the time the fifth attack took place in 1850, the malefactor didn't even bother to bring an unloaded pistol—Robert Pate, formerly of the 10th Hussars, simply ran up behind the Queen's carriage as she was leaving the gates of the palace, and struck her three times on the back of the head with a walking stick. The incident was the more alarming, despite the choice of weapon, because three of Victoria's children were with her at the time. Pate was also sentenced to transportation to Australia.

Lord Palmerston

During 1840s, a decade in which Victoria was principally occupied in bearing one child after another, Alfred underwent a slow transformation from a discontented figurehead consort to the Queen's right hand and de facto private secretary. With Sir Robert Peale, the Tory Prime Minister who succeeded Melbourne, Albert enjoyed a close working relationship, even coming to consider Peale a friend—one of the few which the standoffish Germanic prince ever managed to make in British high society. Until Peale's death in 1850, he and the Prince worked together to repeal the corn and wheat tariffs, though Peale was obliged to cross his own party to establish free trade between Britain and the continent. The repeal of the Corn Laws came to be considered one of the greatest political victories of the Victorian age.

Toward the end of the 1840s, Albert and Victoria had established a close working relationship of their own—the rivalry of the first three years of their marriage giving way to harmony as Victoria chose to subsume more and more of her own "political and personal temperament" in Albert's quest to spread "his German federalist view of Europe." In the analysis of historian A.N. Wilson, "the harder Albert worked... the harder [Victoria] had to struggle to suppress her lack of sympathy with his politics. The simplest way of doing this was to adopt the pose that she was only a wife and mother, only a little woman who did not understand male affairs such as politics.

Sometimes, quite probably, this really was what she felt." Considering how much of her time and energy her children consumed, it was probably easier to give way to Albert when possible, especially since her compliance made them into a formidable team. It was necessary for them to stand together as the 1850s dawned and they faced a new political challenge, one with even more dire potential consequences than the conservative opposition to the repeal of the corn tariffs—namely, the out-of-control behavior of the Whig Foreign Secretary, Lord Palmerston.

After more than a decade of being married to the Queen of England, Albert was accustomed to being consulted, particularly in matters pertaining to foreign policy. The Queen herself, of course, had a constitution obligation to review information and dispense guidance and advice to her ministers. But Palmerston's manner of doing business was entirely antithetical to Albert's methodical, inquisitive, principle approached to the business of government, and he infuriated not just the prince, but also the Queen, by taking actions with serious implications for Britain's relationship with her European allies without informing her or waiting to receive her input. Palmerston, due either to his slapdash way with paperwork, or perhaps a more cunning strategy to keep the royal couple out of the loop when it suited him, routinely failed to submit memoranda to the Queen for inspection before taking action in her name. When called to account for this oversight, Lord Palmerston blamed the disorganization of his secretaries, and promised that the matter would be rectified in the future.

But matters were not rectified. The Foreign Secretary continued to make decisions on his own authority without consulting the Queen, such as when he encouraged Victoria's cousin Leopold to marry the 16-year old Queen Isabella of Spain. Victoria and Albert were both concerned that any perceived British interference in the Spanish succession would placed them on a delicate footing with France, whose king had wished to marry his own nephew to Queen Isabella's sister. Furthermore, the young Leopold had given Victoria his personal assurance that he had no interest in the Spanish throne, so she naturally took it as a grave personal offense when Palmerston encouraged Leopold to break this promise. Nor was this the end of Palmerston's misdeeds. He contravened the Queen's wishes by encouraging the Dutch invasion of Schleswig and Holstein, despite the fact that Victoria and Albert clearly foresaw that Prussia would march to Holstein's defense, creating tensions with Austria and France which eventually led to the Franco-Prussian War and German unification in the 1870s.

Every action Palmerston took seemed to court war in Europe, but there were limits to the Queen's power to check him. She could not personally remove one of her ministers from office—or at least, no monarch had done so in a very long time, and it was unclear what the consequences would be if she tried. The most discreet means of dealing with Palmerston would have involved the Queen making her displeasure known to the Prime Minister and trusting him to act on her behalf. But Sir Robert Peale was killed in 1850 after being thrown from a horse, a tragedy which not only deprived the royal couple of a close friend but also removed from the political playing field the only figure of sufficient gravity who could oppose the enormously popular Palmerston without courting ruin.

Victoria and Albert—especially Albert—began remonstrating with Peale's successor, Lord John Russell, explaining why Palmerston was unsuitable and prevailing upon him to exercise some control over the wayward Foreign Minister. Lord John understood the Queen's feelings, but he was reluctant to take immediate action, since, again, removing a high-ranking minister on no other grounds than that he had displeased the monarch raised sticky issues of constitutional law that the Prime Minister was not eager to grapple with. Yet Palmerston often played the same tricks with him, "forgetting" to copy Downing Street on important foreign communications and later blaming it on his secretaries. Lord John's position was a most uncomfortable one, especially when the Queen grew passionate on the subject: "Did Lord Palmerston forget that she was Queen of England? How could she tolerate a state of affairs in which dispatches written in her name were sent abroad without her approval or even her knowledge? What could be more derogatory to her position than to be obliged to receive indignant letters from the crowned heads to whom those dispatches were addressed—letters which she did not know how to answer, since she so thoroughly agreed with them?" In the Queen's view, "Lord Palmerston often endangered the honour of England by taking a very prejudiced and one-sided view of a question; that his writings were always as bitter as gall and did great harm."

At last, Victoria lost patience with her Prime Minister and resolved to act on her own authority. Baron Stockmar, Prince Albert's political tutor, had dictated a certain memorandum and given it into the Queen's keeping, in case circumstances should ever arise in which she would need to use it. Now the time had come; Victoria recopied the document in her own handwriting and dispatched it to Lord John, instructing him to show it to the Foreign Secretary. It reads as follows:

"[The Queen] thinks it right, in order to prevent any mistake for the future, shortly to explain what it is she expects from her foreign secretary. She requires: (1) That he will distinctly state what he proposes in a given case, in order that the Queen may know as distinctly to what she has given her Royal sanction; (2) Having once given her sanction to a measure, that it be not arbitrarily altered or modified by the Minister; such an act she must consider as failing in sincerity towards the Crown, and justly to be visited by the exercise of her Constitutional right of dismissing that Minister."

"Her Constitutional right" to dismiss Palmerston was arguable—no law is set in stone until it has been tested, argued, and carried out at least once so as to establish a precedent, and no such precedent existed. Yet Lord John had no choice but to dutifully pass the memorandum along to Palmerston, whose reaction to it was typical. Any other Foreign Minister in history, probably, would have resigned upon receiving so pointed a rebuke from the Queen, if only out of a sense of personal embarrassment, or at the very least to prevent a debate on sticky points of Constitutional law from being raised on his behalf. But Palmerston had no such sense of embarrassment. He was elderly, fond of his powerful position, and rather shocked to discover that the little Queen he served contained sufficient mettle to challenge him in this way. So instead of resigning Palmerston merely acknowledged receipt of the message, replying that of course he would comply with its dictums. But when Albert summoned him shortly afterwards for a personal interview to discover precisely what plans Palmerston had made to change the Foreign Office's manner of doing business, Palmerston had no precise information to give him. He was flustered, flushed, and inarticulate in the face of Albert's questioning, and eventually excused himself from the royal interview without having made a single promise or addressed a single one of the prince's concerns.

Lord John Russell threatened and cajoled Palmerston on the Queen's behalf for the rest of the year. But it was not until Louis Napoleon, nephew of Napoleon Bonaparte, made himself

Emperor of France, that the Prime Minister was moved to take decisive action. Neutrality was the express policy of the British government in the face of French political upheaval. For the first decades of the nineteenth century, Britain had been consumed by its war with France; it was imperative that the peace be maintained now. But Lord Palmerston, as liberal abroad as he was conservative at home, could not restrain himself from writing an approving and congratulatory note to the French government on the success of Napoleon's coup. The Queen, when she learned of it, was livid, and Lord John demanded that Palmerston retract the note. Instead, Palmerston wrote a second letter, on the same approving lines as the first. With this, the Prime Minister reached the end of his patience; he dismissed Lord Palmerston from office, and Lord Granville, a protégé of Prince Albert's, was appointed Foreign Secretary in his stead. But Granville was not to keep his office for long. The Whig government fell shortly after Granville's appointment, and he was obliged to give way to Lord Clarendon, a Tory. Palmerston himself, who had been demoted to the Home Office, resigned from the government entirely.

Public outrage ensued. Lord Palmerston was enormously popular with the British people. Without precisely understanding what it was he had done when he was Foreign Minister, the English public perceived him as a strong, redoubtable, quintessentially English statesman along the lines of such legendary figures as Wellington. Palmerston's resignation made the people feel as if their government had been laid vulnerable to the revolutions and upsets shaking the governments of France and Italy. But who had taken Palmerston from them? Foreign elements in the government, acting to weaken the nation from within, must be responsible; and whenever "foreign elements" were mentioned in politics, everyone understood that Prince Albert, who stood in England as *the* foreigner, was implicated. The Prince was not popular in English high society. At the beginning of her reign, when the Queen was unmarried and the protégé of Lord Melbourne, she had been the darling of Whig social circles. But since her marriage, she and Albert had virtually vanished from society. This in itself was not alarming, since the monarch was not required to be a fashionable figure, but Albert's German appearance, his un-English tastes, his disdain for hunting and dancing and drinking after dinner, made him unknowable to his peers—and anything that is unknowable is suspicious. In fact, Palmerston's resignation had nothing to do with Albert, but he was apt to making indiscreet statements in public, implying that "foreign interests" had been to blame for his removal, and this had given rise to the rumors that the Prince had ruined his career.

The time-honored tradition of English xenophobia aside, Albert's very existence raised Constitution questions regarding the role of the monarchy in government which had been allowed to exist in a state of indeterminacy since the late 1600s—and that was without the public's being at all aware of the Queen's memorandum to Lord John, a memorandum drafted by Baron Stockmar, who was as foreign as it was possible to be. Albert's view, crystallized by years of Stockmar's political tutelage, was that in a constitutional monarchy the sovereign had, at the very least, the right to act as a sort of president of a council of ministers. But Parliamentary Whigs, Albert asserted, favored a government by ministry only, which relegated the monarch to a strictly figurehead position. It was their lackadaisical republicanism, not his ongoing debate with Palmerston, which threatened to open the door to popular revolt and the end of the monarchy in England.

Stockmar's memorandum was nothing short of a declaration that "the Crown intended to act independently of the Prime Minister"—not lightly, perhaps, and not without attempting the usual channels first, but when all other recourse failed, the Queen was prepared to assert her right to dismiss ministers who displeased her. This was not so alarming in itself; rather, the problem lay in the fact that the role of the Crown was being re-defined, not by the woman who wore it, but by her husband—a person with no official standing in British law.

But to Albert, his standing and position in the government was perfectly unambiguous. In 1850, he wrote a letter to the Duke of Wellington, declaring that his job was to "sink his own individual existence in that of his wife—assume no separate responsibility before the public, but make his position entirely a part of hers—fill up every gap which, as a woman, she would naturally leave in the exercise of her regal functions—continually and anxiously watch every part of the public business, in order to be able to advise and assist her at any moment in any of the multifarious and difficult questions or duties brought before her, sometimes international, sometimes political, or social, or personal. As the natural head of her family, superintendent of her household, manager of her private affairs, sole confidential adviser in politics, and only assistant in her communications with the officers of the Government, he is, besides, the husband of the Queen, the tutor of the royal children, the private secretary of the Sovereign, and her permanent minister."

In other words, with no precedent to guide him and after struggling with the question for years, Albert had at long last defined for himself precisely what the duties of a male consort must be. Founded on 19th century attitudes regarding the role of women (which included the assumption that "as a woman" there was a "gap" in the Queen's ability to carry out the duties of her office), Albert's view was that it was incumbent in his marital duties to supply all that was "lacking" in his wife. In other words, when man and wife became one flesh, they also, when the wife happened to be a Queen, became one Sovereign.

It was an argument which seemed calculated to sway the male Victorian mindset in its favor. When Lord Palmerston, for reasons of his own, renounced his resignation from office and returned to government duties, the intense public feeling against Prince Albert transformed almost overnight into wholehearted approval. Speeches were made in Parliament upholding his right to advise the Sovereign in any way he saw fit. It was the culmination of Albert's long struggle to take an active role in English politics.

First, he had to convince his wife; that accomplished, he had to convinced the people. Now that his place in government was assured, he turned his eye outwards, his ambitions fixed on a new project: the Great Exhibition of 1851, which would mingle the innovations of English technology, manufacturing, science, and art with the liberating politics of free trade, to demonstrate, "in visible glory before the eyes of an astonished world", the might of Victorian England.

The Great Exhibition of 1851

"The Great Exhibition of the Works of Industry of All Nations" was the grand-sounding title chosen for the crowning triumph of what might justly be referred to as Albert's reign as Victoria's consort. Modeled on the French Industrial Exhibition of 1844 and a number of smaller domestic exhibitions which had taken place in England over the past decade, the Great Exhibition would surpass entirely everything which had come before it, and give rise to a series of copycat exhibitions in various countries around the world over the next fifty years.

The spirit of free trade inspired the international reach of the Great Exhibition. By exhibiting the art, design, and technology of nations around the world in an English setting, Prince Albert and his associates—inventor Henry Cole, artist George Wallace, radical politician Charles Dilke, and others—hoped to encourage a spirit of friendly international competition that would create a spirit of education, innovation, and scientific inquiry in Europe generally. Those who approved of the Exhibition's aims naturally assumed that, as the host country, England would only profit from sharing its innovations with the rest of the world; but conservative elements of society were convinced that the Exhibition would only open the door to hurtful competition for British manufacturers.

The Exhibition was to take place in the Crystal Palace, a temporary yet magnificent structure built in Hyde Park to house the more than 14,000 exhibitions that made up the festivities. Built out of wood, glass, and iron, the Palace might not sound terribly impressive to those of us who are accustomed to towering glass-fronted skyscrapers, but in 1851, no structure like it had ever been seen before, and audiences were accordingly mesmerized. Renowned gardener Joseph Paxton, who designed the famous gardens at Chatsworth, influenced the construction of the Palace; he would later reproduce his designs to create the famous greenhouses that enabled exotic lilies to be grown in Britain. He is credited for popularizing the modular design that allowed the enormous structure to be built in less than a year.

As the date for the opening of the Exhibition approached, critics began to prophesy disastrous consequences for opening Britain's borders to a mob of foreign visitors. Conservatives especially feared that the foreigners would bring with them revolutionary Marxist politics and foment rebellion amongst the British people, or even stage a foreign takeover of the government. King Ernest of Hanover, Victoria's uncle, who had been heir presumptive to the English throne until the birth of the Princess Royal, was a particularly outspoken critic of the exhibition. He wrote that:

"The folly and absurdity of the Queen in allowing this trumpery must strike every sensible and well-thinking mind, and I am astonished the ministers themselves do not insist on her at least going to Osborne during the Exhibition, as no human being can possibly answer for what may occur on the occasion." [Osborne House, on the Isle of Wright, was one of the Queen's country residences—King Ernest's idea is that Victoria might well be assassinated by an angry mob of foreigners unless she left London before the Exhibition began.] "The idea... must shock every honest and well-meaning Englishman. But it seems everything is conspiring to lower us in the eyes of Europe."

Contrary to this paranoia, the Great Exhibition was an astounding success, and only enhanced Victorian Britain's global reputation as a leader in technology and modernity. The Crystal Palace was visited by six million people between its opening on May 1, 1851, and its closing on October 11th of that year—a number equivalent to a third of the entire population of Britain at the time. As many as 42,000 people visited the Exhibition every day.

Queen Victoria wrote an extensive account of the day she opened the Exhibition and witnessed its grandeurs for the first time. Her excitement and enthusiasm mirrored that of the tens of thousands of other guests taking in the sweeping glass walls and curious displays:

"May 1. This day is one of the greatest and most glorious days of our lives, with which to my pride and joy, the name of my dearly beloved Albert is for ever associated! It is a day which makes my heart swell with thankfulness... The Park presented a wonderful spectacle, crowds streaming through it, - carriages and troops passing, quite like the Coronation, and for me, the same anxiety.

"The Green Park and Hyde Park were one mass of densely crowded human beings, in the highest good humour and most enthusiastic. I never saw Hyde Park look as it did, being filled with crowds as far as the eye could reach. A little rain fell, just as we started, but before we neared the Crystal Palace, the sun shone and gleamed upon the gigantic edifice, upon which the flags of every nation were flying. We drove up Rotten Row and got out of our carriages at the entrance on that side. The glimpse, through the iron gates of the Transept, the waving palms and flowers, the myriads of people filling the galleries and seats around, together with the flourish of trumpets as we entered the building, gave a sensation I shall never forget, and I felt much moved...

"The sight as we came to the centre where the steps and chair (on which I did not sit) was placed, facing the beautiful crystal fountain was magic and impressive. The tremendous cheering, the joy expressed in every face, the vastness of the building, with all its decoration and exhibits, the sound of the organ...and my beloved husband, the creator of this peace festival 'uniting the industry and art of all nations of the earth,' all this was indeed moving, and a day to live for ever. God bless my dearest Albert, and my dear Country, which has shown itself so great today. One felt so grateful to the great God, whose blessing seemed to pervade the whole undertaking.

"This concluded, the Procession [opening ceremonies] of great length began, which was beautifully arranged, the prescribed order being exactly adhered to. The Nave was full of people, which had not been intended, and deafening cheers and waving of handkerchiefs continued the whole time of our long walk from one end of the building to the other. Every face was bright and smiling, and many had tears in their eyes. Many Frenchmen called out 'Vive la Reine'. One could, of course, see nothing but what was high up in the Nave, and nothing in the Courts. The organs were but little heard, but the Military Band at one end had a very fine effect, playing the march from Athalie as we passed along. The old Duke of Wellington and Ld. Anglesey walked arm in arm, which was a touching sight. I saw many acquaintances amongst those present. We returned to our place and Albert told Ld. Breadalbane to declare the Exhibition to be opened, which he did in a loud voice saying 'Her Majesty commands me to declare this Exhibition open,' when there was a flourish of trumpets, followed by immense cheering. We then made our bow and left.

"That we felt happy and thankful, I need not say, proud of all that had passed and of my beloved's success. I was more impressed by the scene I had witnessed than words can say. Dearest Albert's name is for ever immortalised, and the absurd reports of dangers of every kind and sort, put out by a set of people the 'soi disant' fashionables and the most violent protectionists, are silenced. It is therefore doubly satisfactory that all should have gone off so well and without the slightest incident or mischief. Phipps and Col. Seymour spoke to me, with such pride and joy at my beloved one's success and vindication after so much opposition and such difficulties, which no one but he with his good temper, patience, firmness and energy could have achieved. Without these qualities, his high position alone could not have carried him through."

From it conception to its opening, the Great Exhibition had taken two years to bring about—a feat which will be more easily appreciated when one compares it to the fact that Olympic hosting cities need four years to prepare for the opening of the games. The Queen's pride in her country and in her husband, whom she credited for the whole thing, bordered on "delirium". Most remarkable of all was the fact that the Exhibition had paid for itself with the revenues it generated, and had even generated a profit of around £165,000. Even the loudest and harshest of the Exhibition's critics were silenced in the wake of its success. And it secured Albert's legacy forever in British history. As the Queen wrote to her uncle Leopold in Belgium, the opening of the Exhibition was "the greatest day in our history, the most beautiful and imposing and touching spectacle ever seen, and the triumph of my beloved Albert... It was the happiest, proudest day in my life, and I can think of nothing else. Albert's dearest name is immortalized with this great conception, his own, and my own dear country showed she was worthy of it. The triumph is immense."

Chapter Four: The Widow of Windsor (1853-1899)

Europe

From October 1853 to March 1856, Britain was immersed in the Crimean War, member nation of a coalition that united England, France and the Ottoman Empire against Russia. The concern of the European powers was that Russia would succeed in toppling the crumbling Ottoman Empire in its entirety, which would give Tsar Nicholas I an uncontested staging ground in the Black Sea for a potential invasion of the continent. The borders of the Russian empire were already vast, and the English were not prepared to tolerate any further expansion.

There was just one problem with England's joining the war effort against the Russians, and that was the state of the English army. It was almost forty years since English troops had fought against Napoleon, and the army had been allowed to fall into disrepair in the mean time. It was feared by some—wisely, as it turned out—that Britain was no longer capable of fighting and winning a war against advanced military powers. Admiral Wellington, the uncontested hero of Waterloo, wanted Prince Albert to take his place as the commander-in-chief of the British army. From Wellington's perspective, the fact that Albert lacked military experience was not as important as the fact that he was a manager *par excellence*—and Wellington, an experienced veteran, knew better than anyone that armies march on their stomachs, and that stomachs are fed by well-managed supply lines. Lord Ragland was appointed commander in chief instead, however. The Crimean was the first war fought after the invention of photography, and it was also the first war reported upon in the newspapers by an official war correspondent; this meant that the public, for the first time in military history, had a front-row seat to "the tens of thousands of young men…killed for no purpose… languishing with disease and in appalling conditions." The war had enormous popular support in the beginning, but as thousands of British soldiers were brutally slaughtered, the tide of public opinion turned. In Parliament, there was an official censure of the Government's handling of the war effort, which led to the Prime Minister's resignation. Much to Victoria and Albert's dismay, he was swiftly replaced by their old adversary, Lord Palmerston.

But the relationship between the royal couple and the new Prime Minister was quite different from what it had been when Palmerston was Foreign Minister. Albert, Victoria, and Palmerston shared an inveterate hatred of the Russians, which gave them unity of purpose. Besides which, carrying out the grave duties of a war-time Prime Minister had a sobering effect on Palmerston, and he became less inclined to give way to the maverick tendencies that made him such a liability in the foreign office. Palmerston promised the Queen that he could negotiate an honorable peace with the Russians and bring an end to the war. By this time, almost half the British soldiers who had been dispatched to fight in the Crimea were dead. Fortunately for everyone, Tsar Nicholas I of Russia died shortly after Palmerston took power, and his successor, the young and liberal Alexander II, was eager to end the war as rapidly as possible. When Lord Ragland died shortly after hostilities were concluded, Prince Albert suggested that the British army be reorganized into two corps under its two most senior generals—a modernizing move that would lead to the British military's regaining its former prowess.

Vicky and Bertie

Albert was not a military man, but as a German, his interests were naturally allied with Prussia, which was well on its way to building the most formidable army in the world. The object of Prussia's militarization was the unification of the German people—bringing all the smaller German states together as a single German nation under the rule of the Prussian king, Wilhelm I. During negotiations for the Treaty of Paris of 1856, which brought the Crimean War to its official end, Albert and Victoria proposed that their fourteen-year old daughter, Victoria, the Princess Royal, should be betrothed to Frederick, the Crown Prince of Prussia, who was twenty-four. Both Victoria and Albert were enthusiastic about the union, for several reasons; not only would it strengthen the bond between their family and their German relations, but it was hoped that the princess would be a force for good in Prussian politics; she was exceptionally intelligent, and had been carefully tutored in principles of constitutional monarchy. Albert's idea was that his daughter would act as a sort of emissary for English liberalism in her adopted country. It was settled that the marriage itself would not take place until Victoria was seventeen, but Prince Frederick came immediately to the royal residence at Balmoral for the formal betrothal ceremony. Frederick, known as Fritz to his family, was a great favorite with his in-laws to be.

The wedding took place at last in 1857, and while the Queen naturally grew quite emotional as the nuptial day approached, Albert was perhaps even more strongly affected. In parting with his eldest daughter, he was losing the child closest to his heart. The Queen had been so young when Vicky was born that she sometimes declared she felt more like her older sister than her mother. Albert felt quite differently. Victoria found it difficult to relate to her intelligent, cerebral daughter, but Vicky was Albert's likeness, his star pupil who mastered every lesson and exceeded every expectation. The great tragedy of Albert's life as a father was that Vicky had been born a girl. Had she been destined to succeed her mother as Queen of England, he would have felt perfectly easy at the prospect of passing the torch to the next generation. But the succession had fallen instead to his second child and oldest son, Albert, the Prince of Wales, called Bertie. And Bertie was as different from Vicky as could possibly be imagined.

Albert had poured his heart and soul into the education and rearing of Bertie. But Bertie was a disappointment almost from his earliest years.

"How tremendous was the significance of every particle of influence which went to the making of the future King of England!" writes Lytton Strachey. "[His father] set to work with a will. But, watching with Victoria the minutest details of the physical, intellectual, and moral training of his children, he soon perceived, to his distress, that there was something unsatisfactory in the development of his eldest son... Bertie, though he was good-humoured and gentle, seemed to display a deep-seated repugnance to every form of mental exertion. This was most regrettable, but the remedy was obvious: the parental efforts must be redoubled; instruction must be multiplied; not for a single instant must the educational pressure be allowed to relax..."

Perhaps it would have been wiser to allow some relaxation in the youthful Bertie's educational curriculum, because the more pressure that was placed on him, the worse he got. This paradoxical effect probably would not surprise any 21st century educator, since as a society we have evolved some understanding of the fact that different children have different learning styles and emotional needs. But Strachey, writing in 1921, speaks of the young prince's failures with a quaint old-fashioned befuddlement:

"It was certainly very odd: the more lessons that Bertie had to do, the less he did them; and the more carefully he was guarded against excitements and frivolities, the more desirous of mere amusement he seemed to become. Albert was deeply grieved and Victoria was sometimes very angry; but grief and anger produced no more effect than supervision and time-tables. The Prince of Wales, in spite of everything, grew up into manhood without the faintest sign of 'adherence to and perseverance in the plan both of studies and life' as one of the Royal memoranda put it which had been laid down with such extraordinary forethought by his father."

By the time Vicky was married to Fritz, Bertie was only thirteen, but he was already beginning to show signs of the sort of man he was destined to become. He was to grow notorious for his numerous, indiscreet sexual affairs, his fondness for nightclubs, his general "inability to tread the path of duty." Albert would not live long enough to see the worst of Bertie's excesses, but Victoria did, and she never stifled a criticism where he was concerned. The fact that the Queen's surviving diaries have been heavily redacted since her death owes a great deal to the desire of her nine children to edit out her unstinting criticisms of all of them—and her diaries probably contained more criticism of the future King Edward VII than of any of the others. "It is indeed a pity," wrote Albert to Victoria in 1856, just before the birth of their ninth and last child, Princess Beatrice, "that you find no consolation in the company of your children. The root of the difficulty lies in the mistaken notion that the function of a mother is to be always correcting, scolding, ordering them about and organizing their activities. It is not possible to be on friendly terms with people you have just been scolding, for it upsets scolder and scolded alike." It is quite possible that the much-chided young Prince of Wales would have been happier if his father had acted on his own advice, for there is no doubt that where Bertie was concerned, Albert was scolder-in-chief.

A blight descends

The days of mad King George III were not so far off that they had been entirely forgotten by members of the older generation who were near the Queen in the late 1850s and early 1860s. She was in for an extremely difficult few years—in March of 1861 the Duchess of Kent would die, triggering an emotional and mental breakdown in her daughter which was only exacerbated by the death of Albert in December of 1861. But even before these deaths, and quite possibly as a partial consequence of the nine pregnancies she had endured in the course of 17 years, Victoria's temperament began to grow quite volatile towards the end of the 1850s. The above letter written by Albert in 1856 provides a hint of this— her temper was growing short, her outbursts more frequent and more vehement, and there were times when she seemed to grow positively irrational. After the birth of Princess Beatrice, Victoria told her doctor, Sir James Clark, that she did not think she could bear to have another child. The physical strain of so many births in a row had undoubtedly taken its toll on her; during her last few deliveries, she had requested her doctors to administer ether through a cloth mask until she was insensible to pain but still conscious enough to obey the order to push. Sir James shared the Queen's concern that another pregnancy would have a bad affect on her health, but he was more concerned for the state of her mind than her body. Her outbursts and irrationalities, he feared, might be early warning signs that she had inherited her grandfather's mental illness. Albert, though less concerned that she might be losing her reason, was nonetheless much alarmed by her sudden explosions of anger. "You have again lost your self-control quite unnecessarily," he wrote to her after a fight in which she had "followed [him] about and continued it from room to room":

"I do my duty towards you even though it means that life is embittered by 'scenes' when it should be governed by love and harmony. I look up this with patience as a test which has to be undergone, but you hurt me desperately and at the same time do not help yourself."

These outbursts and scenes came to a devastating climax after Victoria's mother died. The Duchess of Kent was diagnosed with terminal cancer by Sir James Clark in May of 1859, when Victoria was 39 and the Duchess was 73. Shortly after her diagnosis the Duchess became seriously ill, and it was not certain if she would recover; the crisis induced a sudden change of mind and heart in Victoria, who for years had kept her mother at a careful distance, never entirely able to forgive her for allow Sir John Conroy to dominate their household when Victoria was a child. The Duchess recovered and lived two more years, but the Queen was shaken: "I hardly myself knew how I loved her, or how my whole existence seems bound up with her— till I saw looming in the distance the fearful possibility of what I will not mention." It is a matter of some contention amongst historians and biographers whether or not the Duchess deserved to be kept at a distance from her daughter—but it is clear that once her mother began to grow ill, Victoria blamed herself for having excluded her. Once, shortly after Victoria became Queen, her mother had written to her: "O Victoria, why are you so cold and indifferent with your Mother; who loves you so dearly?" The Queen did not reply to this inquiry—as a rule, she only replied to about one in three of her mother's incessant letters—but it seems certain that the answer would have referenced the failure of the Duchess to protect her young daughter from Conroy's schemes. For many years, it seems that Victoria believed that her mother did not love her at all, and had only wished to use her, as Conroy wished to use her. But as the Duchess approached the end of her life, Victoria seemed to forget all about these past grievances.

As the Duchess's health began to fail, so too did Albert's—though it seems that Victoria did not take his complaints seriously at first, no doubt because he was, comparatively speaking, a young man, and she did not believe he could be in any real danger. To her daughter, now the wife of the Crown Prince of Prussia, Victoria wrote letters that expressed her feelings about marriage that were hardly calculated to encourage a newlywed:

"You say no one is perfect but Papa," she wrote to Vicky, "but he has his faults too…" His supposed ill-health vexed her: "Dear Papa never allows he is any better or tries to get over it, but makes such a miserable face that people always think he's very ill… All marriage is such a lottery—the happiness is always an exchange—though it may be a very happy one—still the poor woman is bodily and morally the husband's slave. That always sticks in my throat." Coming from the Queen of England, such a complaint is striking, and one must weigh the anecdotal evidence that Victoria was suffering depressions against the realities of the status of women in 19th century society. No doubt she had grounds for feeling that she was "bodily and morally a slave", even if she was in poor spirits generally.

When the Duchess of Kent died on March 16, 1861, Victoria was inconsolable. The doctors had not been completely frank with her regarding the state of her mother's health, and to the end she believed that recovery was possible, so the end came as a terrible shock. More shocking still was the emotional process of collecting and reviewing the hundreds of letters that the Duchess had written to her since she was a small child. A.N. Wilson summarizes their affect on the Queen: "It was not possible, as she read these outpourings of maternal affection which cover four decades, to sustain the personal myth that she had been an unloved child... It is not an exaggeration that the recognition of her mother's love unhinged [Victoria], and that the bereavement precipitated something which was far, far worse than her usual 'nervousness'."

There was no one to comfort her, no one to help her bear this devastating emotional burden but Albert, but the state of Albert's health meant that the added strain of supporting his wife through this crisis only weakened him further. It is not certainly known what disease the Prince was suffering from—his stomach was delicate and he had to take his meals separately from the rest of the family because he could only eat certain bland foods, and those only in tiny quantities. It was difficult for Victoria to understand or relate to his sufferings because she had always enjoyed excellent physical health—the fact that she lived through nine pregnancies attests to this. Modern experts have theorized that Albert may have suffered either from abdominal cancer or from Crohn's disease, the latter being a diagnosis that did not exist in the 19th century. Crohn's is an auto-immune disease in which the intestines undergo periodic flare-ups resulting in ulcerations, agonizing cramps, and diarrhea. And Albert was subject to immense mental and emotional strains which tend to exacerbate disorders of this kind. And he refused to take any sort of rest; he was a workaholic by nature, though he was the first to suggest that others, especially his favorite daughter, take no risks with their health, but nurse themselves through the slightest illness until they were again robust.

Albert's fate was sealed by a final domestic crisis which seemed to bleed away the last of his strength: he discovered that the Prince of Wales, Bertie, was embroiled in an affair with an Irish "actress", a common orphan by the name of Nellie Clifden. It was a "most disreputable" business, an open secret in London's gentlemen's clubs, and eventually someone felt obligated to tell the Prince Consort all about it. That the nineteen-year old Bertie should be making a public scandal of himself with such a woman was all the more distressing because his parents were on the verge of arranging his marriage with Princess Alexandra of Denmark—an alliance that would certainly be cancelled by the bride's family if a shadow of a doubt as to Bertie's character were raised.

Albert's personal history made him feel the potential disgrace of his son's conduct all the more keenly. He was himself the child of a divorced couple—his mother had lived openly with lovers and his father had contracted syphilis from affairs with disreputable women. Albert took Bertie's behavior as a sign that all the effort, all the energy he had poured into his son's education was a waste: "all he got for his pains as a dutiful father was the whole succession of sensualists and vulgarians, on both sides of the family, who now leered at him through Bertie's oyster eyes. Here was old George IV with his collection of erotic prints; here was William IV with his ten illegitimate children; here, oh horror, as Albert's own mother Luise…"

Bertie was at Cambridge at the time, and the severely ill and weak Prince Consort felt it his duty to go and see his son personally, "to speak to his son man to man". It was late November; they took a long walk outdoors in a downpour of frigid rain; Bertie, who really was kind-hearted and hated to disappoint his parents, promised his father that he had broken off ties with Nellie and was heartily sorry for the pain he had caused the family. Albert spent the night at Cambridge, wracked with fever and rheumatisms, and by the time he returned to Windsor, "he was a seriously sick man." The date was November 26th, 1861. On December 14th, at 10:50 in the evening, Albert died at home in the Blue Room of Windsor Castle, where both George IV and William IV had breathed their last. The Queen was at his bedside to the very last. Her diary, which contains no more entries for 1861 after this date, reveals the painful deathbed scene:

"Two or three long, but perfectly gentle breaths were drawn, the hands clasping mine, and (oh! It turns me sick to write it) all, all was over... I stood up, kissing his heavenly forehead and called out in a bitter, agonizing cry, 'Oh, my dear Darling!' and then dropped on my knees in muter, distracted despair, unable to utter a word or shed a tear."

Though the Queen would continue to blame Bertie for contributing to his father's death until the end of her life, he was her comfort in that moment. A Colonel Phipps carried her from Albert's bedside and laid her to rest on a sofa in an adjacent room. Bertie came and threw his arms around her: "Indeed, Mama, I will be all I can to you." She returned his embraces, and whispered, "I am sure, my dear boy, you will."

The Widow

In recent years, there has been a growing interest in "the young Victoria", the teenage girl who escaped the clutches of John Conroy and the Kensington System and became Queen at what used to be considered the most interesting age in a young woman's life—the years of her early youth prior to her marriage, when a whole world of possibilities seemed open to her. A recent film in 2009 depicted this era of the Queen's history in loving detail, opening with the famous scene in which the villainous Conroy looms over her sickbed, ending with the triumphant romance between the young Queen and her handsome prince. As of 2016, there is an ongoing miniseries set during the same period of Victoria's life; it takes considerable liberties with history, choosing, for instance, to cast her relationship with Melbourne as a mutual romance. The message is plain: people want to know about Victoria the girl, the pretty princess who became a queen and took her destiny into her own hands.

For this reason, the majority of this book has been devoted to the drama of Victoria's first two decades as Queen: the rocky start to her reign, her flirtations with Lord Melbourne, her anxieties about marriage, her sudden love affair with Albert, her difficulties reconciling her role as an autonomous Queen with her more constricted role as a 19th century wife and mother. The reason that we find these aspects of Victoria's life so interesting now is because they were, for many years, subsumed in the legend that grew up around her after Albert's death. She was a different person after she was widowed, not only to herself and her family, but to her subjects. Half consciously, half unconsciously, she drew a line dividing her life into *before* and *after*. Before, there was Victoria and Albert, the devoted couple with the growing brood of children who learned how to rule England as a team. After, there was the Widow of Windsor, the Queen who wore black mourning dresses until the end of her life, the more or less static symbol of an era, the Empress of India whose very name suggests colonialism, empire, expansionism. The name "Queen Victoria" tends to summon the image of the stout little woman with the drooping jowls and the long black veils, the stiff icon of Victorian photography. A certain degree of imagination is required to associate the Queen with the pretty young princess who fought for independence and autonomy, who redefined the monarchy for the present age. In many ways, it is as if the woman Victoria died with Albert, and the legend of the Queen was born afterwards—a legend that, at least in our popular imagination, began to erase everything that she was before.

But it is important to remember that Victoria was only in her early forties when she lost her husband and retreated from the public view for the next half a decade. She was still young; half her life remained before her. She would not languish in idleness and loneliness forever, an empty vessel embodying duty and propriety. During the second half of her life, she had an empire to maintain, seven children whose marriages had to be arranged, a plenitude of grandchildren who grew up in close proximity to her. She had close, even intimate friendships with men, including her later Prime Ministers, Disraeli and Gladstone, and that famous controversial "favorite" of the Queen, her Scottish servant John Brown. She continued to write in her diaries daily; indeed, her voluminous journals entitle her to the status of an eminent literary figure in an age that flourished with literary geniuses.

This necessarily limited scope of this book does not allow for a thorough study of the last three decades of Queen Victoria's life. Europe, and the world at large, underwent immense geopolitical upheaval between Albert's death in 1861 and Victoria's death on January 22, 1901. There is little separation between the personal and political in the life of a monarch, so it is safe to say that Victoria herself underwent no fewer upheavals during those thirty years. It is said that the young cannot know how the old feel, but the old are to blame if they forget what it was to be young. But those of us who are students of history have a special duty to remember that the old were once young; that the icons peering out from stiff black and white photos in our history books were once children, teenagers, young people struggling with the burdens of adult life before they felt ready to bear them, just as we are, or once were ourselves.

In 1892, Rudyard Kipling, who was not a historian, but a man of letters, wrote a poem entitled "The Widow at Windsor", about the empire being built in the Queen's name, and the soldiers, "Missess Victorier's son", on whose backs that empire was built:

'AVE you 'eard o' the Widow at Windsor

With a hairy gold crown on 'er 'ead?

She 'as ships on the foam—she 'as millions at 'ome,

An' she pays us poor beggars in red.

(Ow, poor beggars in red!)

There's 'er nick on the cavalry 'orses,

There's 'er mark on the medical stores—

An' 'er troopers you'll find with a fair wind be'ind

That takes us to various wars.

(Poor beggars!—barbarious wars!)

Then 'ere's to the Widow at Windsor,

An' 'ere's to the stores an' the guns,

The men an' the 'orses what makes up the forces

O' Missis Victorier's sons.

(Poor beggars! Victorier's sons!)

Walk wide o' the Widow at Windsor,

For 'alf o' Creation she owns:

We 'ave bought 'er the same with the sword an' the flame,

An' we've salted it down with our bones.

(Poor beggars!—it's blue with our bones!)

Hands off o' the sons o' the Widow,

Hands off o' the goods in 'er shop,

For the Kings must come down an' the Emperors frown

When the Widow at Windsor says "Stop"!

(Poor beggars!—we're sent to say "Stop"!)

Then 'ere's to the Lodge o' the Widow,

From the Pole to the Tropics it runs—

To the Lodge that we tile with the rank an' the file,

An' open in form with the guns.

(Poor beggars!—it's always they guns!)

We 'ave 'eard o' the Widow at Windsor,

It's safest to let 'er alone:

For 'er sentries we stand by the sea an' the land

Wherever the bugles are blown.

(Poor beggars!—an' don't we get blown!)

Take 'old o' the Wings o' the Mornin',

An' flop round the earth till you're dead;

But you won't get away from the tune that they play

To the bloomin' old rag over'ead.

(Poor beggars!—it's 'ot over'ead!)

Then 'ere's to the sons o' the Widow,

Wherever, 'owever they roam.

'Ere's all they desire, an' if they require

A speedy return to their 'ome.

(Poor beggars!—they'll never see 'ome!)

It is safe to say that, as the dawn of the twentieth century approached, this was the image of Queen Victoria which was fixed in the minds of her subjects—the all-power, acquisitive, monstrously wealthy old widow who sat atop her empire like a dragon perches atop a hoard of gold. But by 1892, most of the people living in England had been born during Victoria's reign—they could not remember the Regency, or the mad, profligate kings who preceded her, or how unsteady the throne of England had been by the time she came to occupy it. They knew their Queen only as the inventor of the age in which they lived and moved and had their being. So it was natural that they thought of her less as a person and more as a symbol. But over eighty-two years of living, she was many things: an unhappy, lonely child, a brave young woman, a doting lover, a difficult domestic partner, a critical parent, a woman of letters and passions and deep, devoted feelings and correspondingly bitter grudges.

Queen Victoria's last thoughts are unknown to us, because she lay in a coma for two day before breathing her last; but Lytton Strachey theorizes some of the images from her long life which may have passed "in the secret chambers of consciousness" before the darkness descended at last:

"Perhaps her fading mind called up once more the shadows of the past to float before it, and retraced, for the last time, the vanished visions of that long history—passing back and back, through the cloud of years, to older and ever older memories—to the spring woods at Osborne, so full of primroses for Lord Beaconsfield—to Lord Palmerston's queer clothes and high demeanour, and Albert's face under the green lamp, and Albert's first stag at Balmoral, and Albert in his blue and silver uniform, and the Baron coming in through a doorway, and Lord M. dreaming at Windsor with the rooks cawing in the elm-trees, and the Archbishop of Canterbury on his knees in the dawn, and the old King's turkey-cock ejaculations, and Uncle Leopold's soft voice at Claremont, and Lehzen with the globes, and her mother's feathers sweeping down towards her, and a great old repeater-watch of her father's in its tortoise-shell case, and a yellow rug, and some friendly flounces of sprigged muslin, and the trees and the grass at Kensington."

Other great books by Michael W. Simmons on Kindle, paperback and audio:

Elizabeth I: Legendary Queen Of England

Alexander Hamilton: First Architect Of The American Government

William Shakespeare: An Intimate Look Into The Life Of The Most Brilliant Writer In The History Of The English Language

Thomas Edison: American Inventor

Catherine the Great: Last Empress of Russia

Romanov: The Last Tsarist Dynasty

Peter the Great: Autocrat and Reformer

The Rothschilds: The Dynasty and the Legacy

Further Reading

Victoria, A Life, by A.N. Wilson

Queen Victoria, by Lytton Strachey

http://pdfbooks.co.za/library/LYTTON_S
TRACHEY-QUEEN_VICTORIA.pdf

The Memoirs of Baron Stockmar

https://ia601409.us.archive.org/4/items/
memoirsofbaronst01stocuoft/memoirsofbaronst
01stocuoft.pdf

"The Seven Assassination Attempts on Queen
Victoria"

http://www.thesocialhistorian.com/7-
assassination-attempts-queen-victoria/

"The Widow at Windsor", Rudyard Kipling

http://www.kiplingsociety.co.uk/poems_
widowatwindsor.htm

Made in the USA
San Bernardino, CA
02 July 2018